COLLECTED POEMS OF
St THÉRÈSE OF LISIEUX

———

COLLECTED POEMS OF
St THÉRÈSE OF LISIEUX

———

Translated by
ALAN BANCROFT

Poems of St Thérèse of Lisieux first published in Great Britain
by HarperCollins Publishers, 1996 and 1997

This revised and expanded edition, *Collected Poems of
St Thérèse of Lisieux*, first published in 2001 by

Gracewing
2 Southern Avenue
Leominster
Herefordshire HR6 0QF

ISBN 0 85244 547 4

NIHIL OBSTAT:
Father Philip Caldwell, STL

IMPRIMATUR:
Monsignor Michael R. Quinlan, DCL, V.G.
Salford, 1st October 2001

The Nihil Obstat and Imprimatur are a
declaration that a book or pamphlet is considered
to be free from doctrinal or moral error. It is not
implied that those who have granted the Nihil
Obstat and Imprimatur agree with the
contents, opinions and statements expressed.

Typeset by Action Publishing Technology Ltd.,
Gloucester GL1 5SR

Printed in England by
MPG Books Ltd, Bodmin PL31 1EG

CONTENTS

This book is dedicated
with gratitude to
Father John A. Feeley,
and as one stone in the towering edifice of
memory of
Canon Francis J. Ripley

FOREWORD TO THE FIRST EDITION

by Very Reverend Canon Francis J. Ripley

It is with very special pleasure that I respond to Alan Bancroft's invitation to contribute a foreword to his translation of poems of St Thérèse of Lisieux. I must have been in my early teens when Thérèse first captured me. Towards the end of my Daily Missal I discovered her 'Offering of herself as a holocaust to God's Merciful Love'. I read it and was immediately gripped, captivated by it. From then on I recited it every day after receiving Holy Communion. Love of that prayer led me to enquire about its writer. So I read Thérèse's autobiography. That impressed me more than any other book I had read.

If Thérèse captured me, my pursuit of her became one of the dominant elements in my spiritual life. Throughout my student days I read everything I could find about her. A high spot came when Monsignor Vernon Johnson invited me to one of his retreats in Lisieux. I was one of the foundation members of the Association of Priests of Saint Thérèse of the Child Jesus and until his death I maintained a close friendship with Monsignor Johnson.

Thérèse has always guided me, often in quite delicate ways, and I can well recall the guidance having involved, specifically, that same great prayer by which she had captured me as a boy of twelve at school. When I read Alan Bancroft's translation of her poems I experienced a sensation rather like the one I remember when reading the Act of Offering for the first time. The spirit of St Thérèse is all concentrated in that offering of herself as a victim of love which she wrote out and put in the book of the Gospels she always carried around with her, close to her heart. There it was found after her death.

Thérèse's devotion was not only to God's love but to His *merciful* love. The new *Catechism of the Catholic Church* has six quotations from her writings, more than from any of her Saint-sisters. One of the quotations is from her Act of Offering to Merciful Love. In it she says 'I do not wish to amass merits for heaven, I wish to work for Your love alone':

> This rose, *un-petaled now,*
> is, Holy Child! that heart
> (The figure's true)
> Which wants to immolate
> itself – in every part,
> Always, for You.
> (Poem 66)

The emergence of Thérèse as the most quoted of the female Saints in the *Catechism* shows that her influence is not on the wane. The publication of this splendid translation of her poems should help renew real devotion to her. In fact, it should play a part in hastening what bishops throughout the world are asking of the Pope, that Thérèse be declared a Doctor of the Church.[1] I hope, too, that it will make people take to heart Thérèse's words when she said she went to Carmel 'above all to pray for priests'.

Throughout these verses truths vital to our faith, particularly in these days, are stressed over and over again. I have been looking at my book on Thérèse, *All Love* (1961). In it I wrote: 'The whole point of Christian charity is that we love men for the sake of God . . . when the world is inverting the order of the two great commandments given us by God a little nun in Normandy sensationally puts things right again ...':

---

[1] Pope John Paul II solemnly declared her a Doctor of the Church on 19th October 1997.

This, too, I want (before I go
To see my Jesus in His Light):
To win Him countless souls, and so
To love Him more and more . . .
            (Poem 19);

to win him souls

. . . and by the same
Heart's-fire He came to light them by.
    (Poem 34)

Thérèse's assertion that because the Church is the Body of
Christ it must have a heart and a heart burning with love could
well be described as the heart of these poems. Implicit in them,
too, is her famous definition which opens the *Catechism's* treat-
ment of prayer (2558) – 'For me, prayer is a surge of the heart;
it is a simple look turned toward heaven, it is a cry of recogni-
tion and of love, embracing both trial and joy' – and memo-
rable phrases like 'I am not dying, I am entering into life.'

Lovers of Thérèse will find in these poems the singular
beauty, unique freshness and beguiling simplicity which
throughout her writings illuminate the profundity of her 'Little
Way'. Poem after poem sings to me of the Thérèse I have
known and loved since I discovered her Act of Offering. She
shines more brightly than ever for me now.

Her poems add a wonderful luminosity to all else published.
They make this missionary of spiritual childhood knock at the
door of the heart with an apostolic message that is so desper-
ately needed in the sophisticated world of our day. They add to
the vital message of our little Saint elements of strength,
beauty, truth and love which must result in a richly renewed
appreciation. They can only add force to the words of the Bull
of Canonization, 'Faithful flock of Christ, the Church offers a
new and most noble model of virtue for all of you to contem-
plate unceasingly.'

TRANSLATOR'S INTRODUCTION

These are love poems.

When Jean Daujat wrote a book about their author, he called it *Thérèse: la grande amoureuse* – Thérèse: the Great Lover. And Audrey Butler, in a fine phrase used with the poems in mind, has spoken of Thérèse's 'lyric passion for her God'.

But the passionate and the Passion – the blood coughed, the agonized choking, the near-suffocation; whatever (and not necessarily physical) it may turn out to be for oneself – can be complementary though different aspects of a love which best expresses itself *by* and through suffering, not in spite of it. The former, the passionate, is much less important than the unrapturous latter (just as a positive response to 'If you love me you will keep my commandments'[1†], is essentially a matter of will, not emotion). Imitation of Christ must not exclude Christ's Crucifixion: which, though it was accepted – sought, indeed – wholly out of love, was not a luxuriantly emotional occasion when the nails tore through the flesh. Acceptance of suffering on one's own part (and with Thérèse it went further than acceptance) can be a love-token, a love-present worth more than words.

St Thérèse

Marie Françoise Thérèse Martin, Sister Thérèse of the Child Jesus, of the Holy Face, died at the age of twenty-four. She,

[1†] The numbers in this Introduction refer to the Notes beginning on page 240.

whose last words (in ecstasy, as the bystanders said, before she fell back gently in death) were 'Oh . . . I love him . . . My . . . God! . . . I . . . love . . . you!!', she it was who, in great aridity of spirit, had suffered for months an illness as a result of which, towards the end, her stomach was as hard as a rock and tuberculosis affecting her intestines had led to gangrene.[2]

Those who today know Thérèse well, and as a friend, will need no elaboration from me. For those who do not, I advise the reading, not only of her autobiography, *The Story of a Soul*, and the *Collected Letters*, but also of the *Last Conversations*, a record of her words during the final months of her illness, and *St Thérèse of Lisieux, by those who knew her*, containing testimonies to the diocesan beatification tribunal. (Details of these books are on pages 240–241.)

But discard any mental image you have of a soppily sentimental girl. Rather, this was someone tough, in the best sense; intelligent, humorous, deep (simplicity and depth can go together); on any true definition of greatness, a great person, a person *whose response of heart was total*. (Yet we shall hear from her – and it is universally true – that her spiritual achievement, her sanctity, had its continuously flowing well-spring in Another, not herself.)

Thérèse's spirituality

It has been truly said that Thérèse loved, not an ideology but a Person:

> O white Host, whom I love! Oh come to me,
> Come to me, for my heart aspires to You . . .
>
> Hear, Jesus, as in tenderness I cry:
> 'Come to my heart!'[3]

This love was not initiated by her; one's love of God never is so, for God 'loved us first'.[4] Thérèse recognized (as we all should, but do not) that God loved her, sought her, personally.

As well she might be, she was astonished that Christ, true God and true man, not only gives and offers love, but *seeks* it, begs it like a mendicant, in return for His:

> You have, as royal court in Heav'n above,
> The Seraphim – and yet, You beg *my* love . . . [5]

The unreservedness of Thérèse's response was remarkable. She kept nothing back.

'My Love, Divine and little'

'Great is the Lord, and greatly to be praised. Little is the Lord, and greatly to be loved.' Who wrote these words about the Incarnation, I do not know: but Thérèse would have wholly approved of them. For, since her Beloved is both God:

> . . . Grandeur from on high
> Has made me His own abode[6]

and also, astonishingly, One who came down to us as a child in a stable, so Thérèse – like someone turning a jewel this way and that – has to focus, now on one dimension of this unique situation, now on another. God is Father; the Word, co-eternal with the Father and the Holy Spirit, became a child and our brother. Thus, her love for this unique Person, Jesus, is sometimes maternal or sisterly, as when she imagines herself in a boat with the Child and says to him:

> If you want to rest and stay
> As the thunder-rumbles scold –
> Upon me, I beg you! lay
> Your head's little locks of gold.[7]

Much more often (as we shall see) it is she who is the child, wholly dependent on God: that is the basis of her spirituality.

The littleness of God at Bethlehem, the littleness of God in the Eucharist, are for Thérèse one: and in the clear light of her simplicity she draws a practical conclusion for her own conduct:

> Hidden as host of white, You live for me:
> Jesus, for You I'll also hide away![8]

'. . . it is in the Host that I see You crowning Your self-annihilations . . . For the sake of teaching me humility, You cannot lower Yourself any more . . .'[9]

Jesus, the Bridegroom

> That He and I be one . . .[10]

What is to be said of Thérèse's 'constant betrothal-bridal motif', as V. Sackville-West[11] unsympathetically described it?

> And this I loved: the Host of white
> Came in the morning, to unite
> My soul and His, paid court! And with delight
> I opened – flung its doors apart!–
> My heart.[12]

> . . . My Spouse, my Jesus . . .[13]

> I wear already – look,
> it gleams! – His wedding ring[14]

Though, repeatedly, Thérèse speaks of life on earth as an 'exile', yet:

> Now exile can bring no pain,
> With Him – no wish to be free,
> So soft are the bonds that chain
> Ah, this Jealous God and me.[15]

Because Thérèse's vocation was to the life of a Carmelite nun, her use of the nuptial metaphor, which has reference to a union of will and love between the soul and God (of which union on earth there are degrees, degrees of our participation in God's life through sanctifying grace) was established firmly in the setting of the convent: when she speaks of 'spouses of Christ' she means nuns, consecrated in the religious life. But she was familiar with the writings of St John of the Cross, and for him the concept was of wider horizon and referred to a call that is universal. Commenting in the *Spiritual Canticle* on his lines:

> Beneath the apple-tree
> There wert thou betrothed,

he says that the apple-tree[16] 'is the wood of the Cross, where the Son of God ... betrothed our human nature to Himself, *and, by consequence, every soul of man.*'[17] (St Bernard realistically adds that some souls 'are not in need of a Bridegroom but of a heavenly doctor';[18] and, as for those who attain to their destiny, Thérèse herself reminds us that a thimble-glass and a large tumbler can both be full to the brim with 'as much glory as they can take'.)[19]

The nuptial metaphor *is* only a metaphor, of course, though an apt one. For it has not 'entered into the heart of man, what things God hath prepared for them that love him.'[20] Of the perfection of union with God, in heaven – our high and eternal destiny as individuals if we achieve it – St John the Evangelist can only say that 'we shall be like' Him.[21] 'The immense riches that God possesses by nature,' wrote Ruysbroeck, 'we may possess by virtue of love ...'.[22] Christ's Mystical Body, the 'Bride' of Christ, is made up of countless individual members.

Though St Thérèse is a Saint of the ordinary in a way that St John of the Cross is not, we can apply to her Maritain's words about the latter. To her readers, *us*, she reveals, 'depicted with strokes of flame, the real way to tear off and cast aside the ... pretence of our wretched masquerade, telling them in one word for what they have been created.'[23]

On the morning of his execution, St John Fisher said it was his 'wedding day'.

Annihilation of one's own will – Transformation

It is not a marriage of equals, this entry into the 'family' of God, here and in heaven. The disproportion is dizzying, yet not such as should daunt us. To her hesitating cousin, Marie Guérin, Thérèse wrote: 'You seem to me like a little village girl whom a mighty king comes to ask in marriage and who does not dare accept on the pretext that she is not rich enough, or trained enough in the usages of court; without reflecting that her royal fiancé knows her poverty and her weakness much better than she knows it herself ...'[24]

There is no ambiguity about Thérèse's descriptions of her Lover and loved one: He is true God and true man. When still a baby, in the arms of Mary on the flight to Egypt or at Nazareth, He every moment:

> ... upheld the world
> by keeping it in mind.[25]

And, for Thérèse (wholly scriptural, wholly Catholic, in her theology) Christ's sufferings and death made available to us the very life of the Trinity, the 'family life' of God. For one who would love Jesus:

> Father and Son his Visitants shall be ...[26]

By baptism (Thérèse makes St Cecilia say to Valerian):

> The True and Only God will live in you indeed.
> The Holy Spirit ... He will animate you then.[27]

The uniqueness of the other Person in the marriage-betrothal brought an apt response from Thérèse. In recognition of that uniqueness and her creatureship and dependency, she relies utterly on the loving God, the omnipotent. She retains her personality, as she must (and how delightful a one it is!) but gives up entirely what Marmion calls 'the proprietorship' of her activity, her life. In that sense, she wants to be lost in God, as a drop of water loses itself in a great sea. She seeks a total annihilation of her own will: in so far, that is, as it differs from God's will. 'Yes, I want Him to take over my faculties in such a way that I no longer perform any human and personal actions, but actions wholly divine and directed by the Spirit of Love.'[28] In this only is to be found her fulfilment, here as well as in eternity:

> Love's Fire! consume me ruthlessly ... [29]

> Fresh altar-roses, Lord,
>   are gratified to shine –
>   Self-gifts we *see*!–
> Instead of that *I* would
>   (this other dream is mine)
>   Un-petal me ...[30]

Of the Heart of Jesus:

> You know – all my desires to You are known –
> My wish is that I *lose myself in It*.[31]

> Fire burns inside my soul; it came
> My heart – for always! – to endue.
> I walk in Love's enchanting flame.
> It always will consume me through.[32]

> Flame-drawn, the little moth (oh, see!)
> Becomes a flame itself ...[33]

'In order to live in one act of perfect Love, *I offer myself as a victim of holocaust to Your* MERCIFUL LOVE, beseeching You to consume me ceaselessly, letting overflow into my soul the waves of *infinite tenderness* which are contained in You, that thus I may become a *Martyr* of your *Love*, O my God! ... I want, O my Beloved, with each beat of my heart to renew to You this offering an infinite number of times ...'[34]

Centre of reliance

As Blosius pointed out, indignation at one's own imperfections is often the effect of self-love;[35] we are disturbed when the bogus perfection of our pharisaical self-image is shown (by ourselves to ourselves, even) to be less than complete.

Thérèse's self-image is humbler and finer. 'I see my weakness, but it gives me no distress,' she writes in a poem addressed to Mary, the human Mother given to us by God.[36] Thérèse does not belittle sin (that is, offences against God). Much less does she belittle grave sin; rejection of God's love fills her with horror and she has a 'thirst' to 'save sinners' through her suffering. At the same time she distinguishes our sins from our sillinesses and our indeliberate 'faults which do not OFFEND Him' but merely have 'the effect of humbling oneself and making love stronger.'[37] 'I will have the right, without offending the good God, to do little stupid things up to my death, if I am humble, if I stay very little. Look at little children: they never stop breaking things, tearing things, falling down, all whilst loving their parents very, very much.'[38]

Some spiritual persons examine the 'escutcheons' of their past lives and even though the blots have been wholly wiped away by God's forgiveness and absolution (which, rightly, they do not doubt), they nevertheless *torment* themselves at the fact that blots were ever there; almost as though on the self-regarded 'escutcheon' the blots were there still. Thérèse will have none of this:

> Living by Love means banishing all fear –
> All glancing-back to faults of earlier day:
> Of my past sins I see no imprint here,
> Love in a trice has burnt them all away.[39]

xviii

She speaks of the tender God:

> . . . loving me – my frailty no less,
> The whole of me![40]

Paradoxically, a recognition of one's own nothingness and a surrender to the Mercy of God bring liberation, since reliance on God (who can be relied on) replaces the desire for a self-justification that is non-existent, illusory.

During her last illness Thérèse 'saw through the window the setting sun casting its last fires over nature, and the top of the trees appeared all golden. I said to myself then: What a difference if one stays in the shade or, on the contrary, opens oneself to the sun of Love . . . Then, one appears all golden. In reality I am not that, and I would cease to be that immediately if I withdrew myself from Love.'[43] It was impossible, said Thérèse – not difficult, 'impossible'[41] – to do anything of supernatural worth by herself:

> I know, in all our acts of justice, we
> Have nothing that's of value to You, so
> My sacrifices . . . all! as in a sea –
> To give them worth – into Your Heart I throw . . .[43]

She wanted 'to work for Your *Love alone*' (Act of Offering), and she sought a transformation of her love and of her works.[43a] She knew that she needed an 'ascenseur' – an elevator, a lift; a parent who comes specially down from the top of the stairs and carries the infant up.[44] It is St Paul's 'Gladly therefore will I glory in my infirmities, that the power of Christ may dwell in me.'[45] And it is John Henry Newman's:

> Simply to His grace and wholly
> Light and life and strength belong,
> And I love, supremely, solely,
> Him the holy, Him the strong.[46]

'The saints have always had a lively awareness that their merits were pure grace': *Catechism of the Catholic Church*, 2011, quoting Thérèse's Act of Offering.

Her 'little way' is the way of humility; of a child who, knowing its littleness, does not pretend to be big. Humility simply recognizes reality – the reality of who and what God is and who and what we are. Human pride ridiculously struts in unreality, in untruth.[47] 'Littleness', Thérèse insists, is the only way to make spiritual progress; one must descend to ascend[48]: He must increase, I decrease.[49] 'As soon as He sees us really convinced of our own nothingness . . . He stretches out His hand to us; but if we want to try to do some great thing, even under the pretext of zeal, He leaves us alone.'[50]

> 'I . . . am the one who stunts tall trees and
> makes the low ones grow' (Ezekiel 17:24)[51]

Like Elizabeth of the Trinity after her, Thérèse said that 'our mission is to forget ourselves . . .';[52] her heart, she wrote, had to be 'wholly empty of me.'[53] (But one loved by God is not a 'no-one', and that is the true basis of self-esteem.)

Thérèse's loving was entirely by grace and entirely by free will (for grace perfects nature and does not destroy the freedom of our wills). But even the love she gives to God, Thérèse regards as having come in the first place from God, who asks for the love of our free wills in return. I will love You, she says to Jesus:

> with such Love – the very same –
> As I received, Eternal Word, from you.[54]

The thirteenth-century mystic, Blessed Angela of Foligno, wrote: 'And I understood that He desired the soul to love Him, with that same love with which He loved the soul, according to her power and strength' – her capacity – 'and that, *according to her desire*, so would He fill her up' as a vessel is filled. '. . . I saw I had nothing good belonging to me. And in that way I saw that it was not I who loved, however much I might see myself to be in love, but that the love was God's alone, with which He reunited himself, and then conferred more and more ardent love than before; and I had a great desire to become one with this love.'[55]

Confidence in Divine Mercy – Spiritual Childhood – Surrender

'Trust' – confidence – and 'total *abandon*'[56] were the words Thérèse used to summarize her 'way of spiritual childhood'. (The French *abandon* is almost untranslatable. As used by Thérèse it means the reckless, the unreserved, entrusting to God of oneself and what happens to one.) We can see why she used these words; they describe the relationship of a child – a helpless, *little* child – to its loving parents. 'To stay little is . . . to expect everything from the good God, as a very little child expects everything from its Father. It is not worrying about anything . . .'[57]

She holds out 'empty hands'[58] as a child in its simplicity does. 'I know well that I shall never be worthy of what I am hoping for; but I stretch out my hand to You like a little beggar' – a child with its hand out – 'and I am sure you will grant my wishes fully, for You are so good.'[59] For her, prayer is 'an upsurge of heart, a simple look thrown towards Heaven,'[60] habitually; and Jesus, she said, gives her what she needs spiritually, as she needs it, without her knowing how.[61]

God as a father, God as a lover . . . all the emphasis is upon tenderness and Divine Mercy. His Love in fact is All-mercy; stooping lovingly to our weakness, gratuitous. God is Justice also (hence her concern at and for sinners who reject Him). But justice and mercy are not separated: 'What a sweet joy to think that the good God is *Just*; that's to say, that He takes our weaknesses into account, that He knows perfectly the frailty of our nature.'[62]

Using words which on first publication after her death were

attributed (dubiously) to St Augustine, Thérèse calls *abandon* 'the delicious fruit of love':

> It gives me, here below,
> Repose – a sea of peace . . .[63]

> My Saviour, I'm caressed,
> I'm lulled, upon the breast
> Of You, my All.[64]

She is a child, loved, 'dandled'[65] upon the knee; a lover, *loved*:

> One sees it – on the wings of prayer
> The ardent heart is soaring high,
> As when the lark – in upper air –
> Sings as it rises in the sky.[66]

> Here, in your hearth, I stay and will not move;
> Singing within your fires in restfulness:
>   'I live by Love!'[67]

Active response

But it would be wholly, ludicrously, wrong to think of her as lapsing into quietism;[68] a child sitting back on the shore and letting the waves of love lap over her. Ten thousand times, no! As Victor Sion[69] says, 'She never uses her weakness as an excuse to avoid an effort.' (A violinist, who at first may practise laboriously, still requires to make a *great* effort – for correctness of fingering and precision of bowing – even when he is relaxedly surrendering himself to the music.)

One of Thérèse's poems, 'The Story of a Shepherdess become Queen' (ostensibly about the novice, Sister Marie-Madeleine, but every poem says something about Thérèse herself) speaks of the shepherdess hearing the call to Carmel, and:

> Hearing, the shepherdess at once
> In joy, sets out and will not stop;
> Helped by her Mother, Mary – runs . . .[70]

'*Runs*' . . . Though it is translator's poetic licence which admits that precise word, not explicitly in the French, there could be no better word[71] to characterize Thérèse's response in love; and not only as regards her entry to 'the little Carmel of Lisieux'. What marked the whole of her life there was her alacrity and (in the words of her sister, Pauline) 'a most generous attentiveness to seize every opportunity of doing acts pleasing to God.'[72]

Poverty, obedience, virginity, all involved renunciation; but the renunciation was eager, not grudging, there was no 'I wish I did not have to':

> But no created being could I find
> Who here on earth would love me deathlessly . . .[73]

What is to be seen in her, daily, is not passivity, not formality only, but what Monseigneur Guy Gaucher[74] has called 'the dynamism of love'. In her day, no doubt, the Lisieux Carmel's general observance of the letter and spirit of the Rule under Mère Marie de Gonzague – a Prioress so severe in some things – was not all it should have been. But she, Thérèse, has her own promptings of heart; she is there to love; and, for her, love means giving without reserve:

> . . . I have stopped all counting up. I see
> That when one loves, one doesn't measure out![75]

> You want my heart – it's here! I utterly
> Cede my desires to You . . .[76]

And (one says again) not only in passive acceptance:

> Come sword or fire, next *Him* I'll stay serene –
> I'll rush to the arena fearlessly . . .[77]

Of the Blessed Virgin:

> . . . I would strive, but sing as she![78]

Nor is this simply rhetoric. In little things and great, Thérèse showed her love actively and in practical ways. Every little external act, done as well as she could, every hidden sacrifice, great or little, was – not self-directed perfectionism, but – a love-present from her to God. For her, obedience to the Rule, obedience to her religious Superior (even an idiosyncratic Superior like Mère Gonzague) was obedience to God, whom the Superior represented. This is why, for example, when engaged in writing she ends in mid-phrase[79] on the bell ringing. And whilst words were important to her (one who is in love cannot stop talking about the beloved), words alone would not do: she had to *prove* her love for Christ in every-thing, including loving her fellow-nuns with Christ's love, even (indeed, especially) those few individuals who, on the natural level, set her teeth on edge by their mannerisms.[80]

She did not think up artificial penances for herself; as with us, there were plenty to hand in her daily living. In her hidden spiritual life she wanted to make use of every opportunity that came her way. At the age of fourteen, she wrote, she had wished 'to *love* Jesus *passionately*, to give Him a thousand tokens of love whilst I still could.'[81] This wish never left her. Sister Thérèse, said one of her novices, 'transformed all her actions, even the most insignificant, into acts of love.'[82]

She does not count up her good deeds. 'Give away your [spiritual] goods in the measure you get them.'[83] What she is concerned to do is 'to abandon herself, to give herself up, without keeping anything, not even the joy of knowing how much the bank is paying out.'[84]

She loved the Church: she wished, by uncompromising obedience to Christ's Mystical Body on earth, to love and obey Christ. One of her novices expressed such a firm belief in her Little Way that if the Pope himself 'were to tell me you had been mistaken, I couldn't believe him.' Thérèse replied

bluntly, 'Oh! You should believe the Pope above all ...'[85]
(One could do with more of that among Catholics today.)

'To slake the burning ...'

Though the love which she expresses by the actions of her daily
life is for Christ personally, the relationship is not restricted to
'I – You': her love of Him radiates towards others, *for* Him.
She offers her daily sacrifices for priests, for missionaries; she
is apostolic and strives to gain grace for others:

> That Blaze from Heav'n! – into my soul it came:
> I want to spread its burnings all about ...[86]

> I came to Carmel – why?
> *To people Heaven* ...[87]

> The more I feel Your Flame,
>   the more I've got to do
> To slake the burning. How?
>   In giving souls to You![88]

> This harvest-gift of love –
>   with souls for grapes ...[89]

Again looking back on her feelings at fourteen, Thérèse wrote:
I wanted to give my Beloved to drink and I felt myself
consumed with a *thirst* for *souls* ...'[90] 'It was a true exchange
of love ... the more I gave Him to *drink*, the more the thirst
of my poor little soul increased and it was this ardent thirst He
gave me as the most delightful draught of His love.'[91]

'Delightful draught'! Lest anyone should think that her life
in Carmel was packed with perpetual ecstasies, one has here to
stress that rather was it one of daily aridity and worse: for a
period, the desolate absence of any *feeling* about the very exis-
tence of life beyond the grave, utter darkness. There was 'a
wall reaching right up to Heaven, shutting out the stars.'[92]
But:

> . . . adoring You
>   in dark but loving state,
>   I'll see You when it's dawn,
>   O Jesus! – I will wait.[93]

In her darkness and trial[94] she had lost feeling, not faith. Lacking consolation, she sang 'simply what *I will to believe*' when she sang in her poems 'of the happiness of Heaven, the eternal possession of God.'[95] She was in a 'black hole,' soul and body,[96] (and one should not minimize the desolation and horror of it), but nevertheless, way down, 'in an astonishing peace'.[97]

Suffering

When Thérèse wrote that her 'joy' was in suffering for Christ, she did not mean (in her own phrase) *'felt* joy.'[98] She meant 'peace'; and 'To suffer in peace it is enough to will, very much, everything that Jesus wills.'[99] Writing to her sister, Céline, she said: 'He would rather see you stub yourself against the stones of the path by night than walk in broad daylight along a road made colourful with flowers which could slow your advance.'[100]

Describing her First Communion, Thérèse remarked that at that stage Jesus made no demands of her; there had been 'no struggles, no sacrifices',[101] no physical suffering. Later it was otherwise; Monseigneur Gaucher, in his book *The Passion of Thérèse of Lisieux*,[102] has given us a moving description. On the one hand she never sought suffering, of herself and apart from God: 'I am very glad I have never asked the good God for anything;[103] that way, He is forced to give me courage.'[104] If I were to ask for sufferings, these would be my sufferings, *mine*; I would have to bear them alone, and I've never been able to do anything alone.'[105]

And yet, since the more suffering came her way, the more she could prove her love (and the more fruitful her apostolate of grace would be) – in that sense, and for those reasons, she desired more suffering; she uses the word *réclamer*, ask for, claim, even beg for:

> I ask for suffering. The Cross
> I love – desire! Ah, well you know –
> To save one soul from final loss
> A thousand deaths I'd undergo![106]

Thérèse's attitude to suffering is well summarized in the quotation from Père Jamart given in the notes to Poem 44, on page 149. Her motives, varied but related, all spring from love:

> It's in the Winepress – Suffering –
> That I'll be proving what I say ...[107]

> ... *That suffering has charms* my heart knows too;
> One can save sinners – through the Cross, this is.[108]

Suffering was not sought – much less is it permitted by God – for its own sake. Among its mysterious attributes is the fact that through our sufferings (which pass) we can participate voluntarily in Christ's saving work. In her daily life as a Carmelite, Thérèse offered herself especially for this. 'Jesus,' she wrote, 'made me understand that it was through the cross that He wished to give me souls' – and she to give souls to Him – 'and my attraction for suffering grew in proportion as the suffering increased.'[109] Loving Him, she loved others in seeking, above all, to make them love Him too.

She desired suffering as a way of returning love to One who on earth had suffered for her:

> To be like You is my desire,
> So what I ask is suffering ...[110]

> To suffer, silently, so I'll
> Give Jesus comfort – that's my will.[111]

To 'give Jesus comfort': as though, in His agony in Gethsemane, she would stretch out her hand to Him and say, 'I am here.'

Thérèse was 'Sister Thérèse, of the Child Jesus, *of the Holy Face*'. That last description evoked for her a picture of the thorn-crowned Man of Sorrows, and she sought especially to suffer like Him in order to accomplish His will to save souls.[112]

Read Manuscript B in the autobiography for a glowing exposition of Thérèse's vocation: love. Read the *Last Conversations* to see how she has come to a state in which she wants – not just accepts, positively wants – only what her Loved One wants. The scales of her own wishes are in equilibrium between dying soon or living longer . . . whichever He wills.[113]

Fulfilment

The only true fulfilment of a human being is eternal possession of God whose heart-filling loveliness does not, cannot, satiate.

'The loving soul, for the sake of greater conformity with the Beloved, cannot cease to desire the recompense and reward of its love for the sake of which it serves the Beloved, otherwise it could not be true love . . .' (St John of the Cross, *Spiritual Canticle*).[114]

From her sick-bed, during her excruciating last illness, Thérèse could occasionally hear music coming from somewhere in Lisieux. 'This evening,' she said to her sister, Pauline, 'I heard some music in the distance, and I was thinking that I would soon be hearing incomparable melodies . . .'[115]

'Soon Faith will take and tear apart her veil . . .'[116]

'Arise, make haste, my love, my dove, my beautiful one, and come. For winter is now past, the rain is over and gone. The flowers have appeared in our land . . .'[117]

Thérèse wanted, she said, 'to die of love,' but 'To die of love is not to die in transports.'[118] Among her last words were, 'All I have written about my desire for suffering is quite true; I do not regret my being delivered up to Love . . .'[119] 'Oh! I wouldn't want to suffer for a shorter time!'[120] And then, at her last moment (like the sun-burst of sound in Elgar's *Gerontius* when the human soul glimpses God face to face): 'Oh! ... I love him ... My ... God! ... I ... love you!'[121]

> You'll see Him gaze at you – the night
> Will be ablaze that once was black!
> You'll fly to Heav'n, in high delight,
> With nothing now to hold you back.[122]

A remarkable statement: 'Until the end of the world ...'

And yet her 'rest' in Heaven, is an active one! On the morning of 17 July 1897 – she had just coughed up blood – Thérèse had said: 'I feel I'm about to enter into rest. But I feel above all that my mission is about to begin, my mission of making God loved as I love Him, of giving my little way to souls. If God grants my desires, my Heaven will be spent on earth until the end of the world. Yes, I want to spend my Heaven doing good on earth. This isn't impossible, since from the very bosom of the beatific vision the angels watch over us. I can't throw myself into a spree of enjoyment, I don't want to rest as long as there are souls to be saved ... But when the Angel will have said, "Time is no more!", then I shall rest, I shall be able to enjoy myself, because the number of the elect will be complete and all will have entered into joy and into rest. My heart thrills at this thought.'[123]

Hans Urs von Balthasar comments on this extraordinary statement as follows: 'Thérèse rediscovers the ancient patristic conception of heaven, one to some extent shared by the Middle Ages and according to which the saints in heaven are in a transitory state until the Last Judgement. Not until all the members of the Mystical Body are gathered together can the whole Body of Christ rise again; not until the last of the awaited brethren enters into the Kingdom can the heavenly throng cease to bend over the earth with care.' (But 'even this transitory state before the Last Judgement is really and truly heaven', and Thérèse does not doubt that, any more than the early Christian Fathers did.)[124]

Thérèse is, as it were, an active, dynamic saint; demonstrative, often, to those who ask her for things. The huge number of spiritual and physical cures and other remarkable answers attributable to her intercession seems certainly to be a Divine confirmation of a mission to articulate and then to spread her 'little way', rooted as it is in the Gospel.

The poems and the translations

Thérèse's poems were written between February 1893 and July 1897, the year of her death. Her fellow-nuns in the Lisieux convent knew she wrote poems; she wrote some of them for individual members of the community who had asked her to express their own ideas in verse. (Even those poems are rich in Thérèse's spirituality: the developed thoughts are hers.) Yet her fellow-nuns — other than her sisters, Pauline, Marie and Céline, and Mère Marie de Gonzague — had no idea,[125] until after her death, that Thérèse had written her autobiography (on which she set to work from religious obedience).

Among English-speaking readers today, the position is reversed, almost. There are good English translations of the autobiography, but for those who do not read French the poems are virtually unknown, except through prose translations of short extracts or verse translations of the more celebrated of the poems. In the early part of this century, two English verse translations of the greater number of those poems which had appeared in French editions of the autobiography (from 1898 onwards) emanated from translators in the United States. Both these verse translations are now out of print, and in literary terms neither was an outstanding success.

Not that Thérèse's poems in the original French are regarded as great *literary* works by French critics: in the latter's view this line is '*faible*', that phrase 'maladroit'. My English ear can neither confirm nor deny the validity of such judgments, but if they are correct, then I simply say 'So be it.' For me, as for those same French critics, it is in their content that the real interest of the poems lies. I think they are great love-poems, and so distinctive as to be incomparable.[126]

My previously-published *Poems of St Thérèse of Lisieux* contained translations of fifty poems. The present book contains 72 translations. The poems here translated consist of: all the poems, 62 in number, contained in the French critical edition, *Un Cantique d'Amour*, together with my selection of ten poems from Thérèse's plays. The translations here published for the first time are Poems 3, 7, 8, 10, 12, 13, 15, 17, 18, 28, 31, 36, 37, 42, 49, 50, 52, 53, 54, 65, 70 and 71, to use the numbering of the present book. Of these newly-published translations, all except Poem 15 (a 'poem from a play') are of poems first published in *Un Cantique d'Amour* (Paris: Les Éditions du Cerf et Desclée de Brouwer, 1979). It was for copyright reasons that they were not included in my earlier book, but they are published here under a permission now obtained from ICS Publications, Washington DC, and Cerf DDB, Paris, for which I desire to express my gratitude.

The translations included in the earlier book were, in most part, from texts originally published not long after Thérèse's death. Those texts had been 'improved' (a word which need not in every case be used ironically) by Thérèse's sister Pauline, Mother Agnès de Jésus. All the translations in the present book are from the critically-restored Theresian texts. Additionally, in many places where the French does not differ between the two versions I have revised my former wording. As far as any mere translations can be so, I would like the trans-lated versions in the present book to be regarded as my defini-tive text.

Un Cantique d'Amour did not include the poems which Thérèse wrote for the 'pious recreations', the name given to the plays (some in prose, some in verse, some a mixture of the two) which she composed for the nuns to act in the Lisieux Carmel on feast-days. Certain of those poems appeared in the appendix to *Histoire d'une Ame*. A critical edition of all the plays was published in 1985 under the title *Théâtre au Carmel* (Paris: Cerf DDB).

References to 'PN' (*poésie numéro*) and 'PS' (*poésie supplémentaire*) are references to the numbering in *Un Cantique d'Amour*. References to 'RP' (*récréation pieuse*) are references to the numbering in *Théâtre au Carmel*. The date given after each poem is the date or approximate date stated in those works; either the date or approximate date of composition or the date of the occasion for which it was composed.

To the French and U.S. publishers named above I am happy to give acknowledgement, also, in respect of short quotations, in my own translation, from French material still in copyright which I use in the commentary to illuminate Thérèse's thought and/or to point to parallels between the poems and other works of Thérèse. I make grateful acknowledgement also to the Office Central de Lisieux in respect of short passages translated by me from the manuscript autobiography published by them. I acknowledge in their individual places the sources of short quotations from other copyright material.

The present book is not a critical edition. It aims at conveying something of the 'music' of Thérèse's hymns of love.

Principles of this translation

Thérèse's poems are natural and unsophisticated – often almost conversational – even where her chosen phraseology is stylized and 'poetic'. I have tried to reproduce this in the translations, whilst retaining, I hope, a feel of the period. The translation is not always literal, but my aim has been to reproduce Thérèse's thoughts with exactitude. My judgment may be at fault, but if I have omitted any word or phrase it is because I thought it inessential to her meaning; if I have included in the English something not explicitly in the French, it is because I thought that my words followed naturally from the actual French words.

The rhyme-*scheme* of each translation is exactly that of the French original. I have followed Thérèse's metres too, to this extent at least: that each line has the same number of syllables as in the French. Of course these English verses, with their traditional regularity of stress, are aimed at the English ear. Except in the case of the alexandrines, I have not sought systematically to reproduce the caesurae or internal breaks of rhythm found in the French. I add that where lines of (say) eight syllables in the French could conceivably be translated as trippingly anapaestic three-stress lines or as more stately four-stress lines, I have preferred the latter. I have treated each line-ending 'e' as mute.

These are the poems of a young woman. As I have done in the translations, Thérèse used exclamation marks frequently (though mine in the English are not necessarily in the same places as hers in the French); and when she underlines, italicizes, she does it in order to emphasize the importance of something already made clear, whereas generally[131] I have italicized where I thought it necessary to bring out the meaning itself. However, the parenthetic style of some translated passages and the practice of having an unimportant word at the end of a line (as a kind of springboard for the line which follows), are mine and not hers.

It may not be out of place to say how I came to embark on the translations. When attending Monsignor Francis Horsfield's pilgrimage-retreat in Lisieux in 1992, I was seized with a desire, an impulsion, to translate the poems (which at that stage I had not even read). On the way home to England – as, with my wife, I climbed the steep hill to the Chapel of Notre Dame de Grâce at Honfleur (where, in July 1887, Thérèse, accompanied by her father and her sisters Léonie and Céline, prayed that she might be allowed to enter Carmel at an early age) – I was already 'tasting' in my mind English phrases that might translate a particular French stanza, picked at random, from poem 26, *Vivre d'Amour*.

Acknowledgements

I wish to express my most grateful thanks to successive Mother Prioresses of the Lisieux Carmel and the respective Sisters in charge of the Theresian Archives; the Office Central de Lisieux; Father John A. Feeley (formerly of The Catholic University of America, Washington, D.C.), whose presence in Lisieux was truly providential and whose assessment of the translations, and advice, were so valuable. I acknowledge how much I owe the late Canon Francis J. Ripley and the Community of the St Helens Carmel, for their help, encouragement and prayers.

I am deeply in debt to Audrey Butler who, with her husband Arnold, read the translations in typescript at an early stage, and who both lifted my spirits through her reaction to them and helped me by her constructive suggestions. Judith Swarbrick, as librarian, and the Preston Carmel by the loan of books, assisted me much. I acknowledge the assistance of good friends in France, particularly in the *Service Accueil* of the Pilgrimage Office, Lisieux, as in the Carmel itself, so redolent of the spirit of Thérèse.

Finally, I would like to record my delight at one fact. The late Dr Thomas Holland, former bishop of the Salford diocese, where I live (I had the pleasure of talking with him whilst the earlier work was in preparation) met Thérèse's sisters Pauline and Céline, not in the pages of a book but in actuality; in 1944, at the liberation of France, when he was a naval chaplain and they had just returned to the Lisieux Carmel from their temporary refuge in the crypt of the Basilica.

I feel, somehow, that over the months of translating I have had the honour of meeting Thérèse almost no less personally.

Feast of SS John Fisher and
Thomas More, 1995
Revision, April 2001

NOTE TO THE READER

Pronunciation

Words like 'flower' which could be one syllable or two are pronounced as the metre dictates. Thus in Poem 1, stanza 3 (line 1) 'Flower' is monosyllabic: but by the time one reaches stanza 4 (line 5) that word has opened out into two syllables, like the very bloom it describes.

A word like 'flower' at the end of a line (as in stanza 2) is to be pronounced as a monosyllable.

As with words which could be one syllable or two, so with words which could be two syllables or three, etc. In the same poem, the metre dictates, for example, that 'radiance' (which in other places might be two syllables) shall in stanza 1 be an expansive three syllables, and that 'Sanctuary' in stanza 5 shall be four.

Some words, e.g. 'Heaven' (a word which appears many times in Thérèse's poems) are printed either 'Heaven' or 'Heav'n', to make their pronunciation clear at a glance.

Layout of lines

As in the French, some of the lines are *alexandrines*, consisting of twelve syllables (six English feet). There is a break of rhythm, near-imperceptible or longer, at the end of the sixth syllable (third foot).

These regular breaks of rhythm are signalled in two ways.

Where an entire poem or an entire stanza is made up of alexandrines, the break is indicated by the symbol ', as in Poem 2. Otherwise, it is indicated by the splitting of the line, three feet upper, three feet lower, as in Poem 6.

Key

To the Notes at the foot of each poem, the following key applies:

Aut.	Thérèse's autobiography
l.	line
lit.	literally
Ms.	Manuscript
St.	Stanza

POEMS

1. THE DIVINE DEW or THE VIRGINAL MILK OF MARY

1   My gentle Jesus, on Your Mother's breast
    I see You, as a *radiance* of Love!
    That mystery, whose depth can not be guessed,
    Made You an exile from Your Home above.
    Ah, let me hide where, in that veil, You are
    Removed from mortal gaze; let it be giv'n
    To me that close to You, O Morning Star
    I'll find in it a foretaste, here, of Heav'n.

2   Since first – at break of dawn's awaking-hour –
    A sudden flare of sun the darkness rends,
    The tender bud that's turning to a flower
    Is waiting till a precious balm descends.
    It's *dew*, the kindly dew! – when morning breaks,
    What freshness then this moisture brings about!
    Producing sap abundantly, it makes
    The budded petals start to open out.

3   You, Jesus, are the Flower just open new –
    I watch Your first awaking and see this.
    You, Jesus! – that delightful Rose is You:
    In that vermilion bud, what grace there is!
    Your sinless Mother, rocking You to rest,
    Makes of her arms a royal throne for You.
    What is Your gentle sun but Mary's breast?
    What other than the Virgin's milk, Your dew?

4 My Love, Divine and little! I can see
The future in Your face, dear Brother: how
You soon will leave Your Mother's side, for me:
Love presses You to suffer, even now.
But on the Cross, full-opened Flower! You
Afford me of Your morning Scent a sign:
I recognize what this is – Mary's dew,
The Virgin's milk, this is . . . Your Blood divine.

5 Dew, hidden in the Sanctuary! where
The angels wonder, and their joy is told;
In offering to God their soaring prayer,
They keep repeating, like St John: 'Behold!'.
The Word-made-Host – ah, yes, behold Him who
Is Lamb, and Priest Eternal. We are fed
The Son of God, who's Son of Mary too:
The Virgin's Milk, this is . . . the Angels' Bread.

6 It's glory that the Seraphs feed upon –
Pure happiness they have, in Paradise.
But I'm a child, and weak; Communion
Brings just the image *milk* before my eyes.
That's right for childhood, though – and to out-tower
All else, the Love of Jesus a delight.
O tender Love! Unfathomable Power!
The Virgin's milk, this is . . . my Host of white.

Notes

PN 1

2 February 1893, Feast of the Purification

'. . . the forget-me-not need only half-open, or rather lift up its wreath of petals, in order that the *Bread of Angels* may come like a Divine Dew to strengthen it and give it all it lacks' (Thérèse, letter to Sister Marie of the Trinity, June 1897).

Thérèse's first poem. She has been in Carmel since April 1888. Mère Marie de Gonzague is Prioress, but is about to be succeeded in that office by Thérèse's sister, Pauline (Sœur Agnès de Jésus). Another Thérèse in the community, Sœur Thérèse de Saint-Augustin, has a strong personal devotion to the Holy Infancy, the babyhood of Christ. She asks Thérèse to write a poem on the subject. According to her account, Thérèse at first hesitates: 'I know nothing about poetry . . . I don't know if it's the will of God.'

2. JOAN AT DOMRÉMY

(from a play about Joan of Arc)

After hearing, in the fields, her voices –
St Catherine, St Margaret and St Michael
– Joan delivers her response

For love of You, my God! ¹ for that alone I go –
Depart my father's house, ¹ and parents very dear –
For You, I go to war! ¹ I leave my vale, and, oh,
The lovely village-bell, ¹ the flock I guarded here.
I'll lead the *army* now, ¹ and not these lambs of mine,
No longer shall I play ¹ with pretty flowers, Lord.
My joy, my eighteen Springs, ¹ I give You. As a sign –
To please You, God, this hand ¹ will reach out for a
    sword.

My singing-voice, that joined ¹ the breeze that rose
    and fell,
10 Must, like a steeple-clang, ¹ above the shouting rise:
No more the dreamy sound ¹ of that uncertain bell –
For, louder, I shall hear ¹ a people's battle-cries.
Yes! sacrifice I love. ¹ The cross is my desire:
Ah, call me now for this – ¹ to suffer! Here am I.
To suffer, loving You! ¹ With joy I am on fire.
O Jesus, my dear Love, ¹ for You I want to die.

6

Notes

RP1 (extract)

21 January 1894, Feast of St Agnes

On Sister Agnès's election as Prioress, Thérèse has been given the task of teaching the novices, nominally as assistant to Mère Marie de Gonzague who has become Novice Mistress. The poems now become more frequent. Thérèse often used to compose them in her head during the day. She then did not put them on paper until the free time between Compline and Matins, and 'it was not without extreme difficulty that I remembered, at eight in the evening, what I had composed in the morning.' (*Conseils et Souvenirs.*)

This poem is from Thérèse's first play, *The Mission of Joan of Arc, or The Shepherdess of Domrémy hearing her Voices:* see Translator's Introduction, pages xxxi–xxxii. There are obvious parallels to Thérèse's entering Carmel. She leaves her father, still at Les Buissonnets, and goes to war, to a voluntary and loving martyrdom.

l. 10 Lit. 'Must soon ring out, from the very heart of the battle.'

3. TO OUR MISTRESS AND DEAR MOTHER, TO CELEBRATE HER SIXTY YEARS

*Mother Marie de Gonzague was 60
on 20 February 1894*

1   This *is* a Happy Birthday; how
We celebrate with joy! and when
We fête our tender Mother now
Let's sing our love and sing again!

2   For sixty years You've watched her here,
O Jesus (God and Nourisher!).
To You this flower is very dear.
Your graces are bedewing her.

3   Herself a flower whose scents upbear
Hearts gained for You, this guide of ours
Has gathered, in the valley there –
Oh what a splendid crop of flowers!

4   And in our Home Above we'll see
What recompense for her You've stored! –
Those flowers she gathered here will be
The plaited crown of her reward.

5   This Mother (whom we call Your *Rose*)
Directs us all, her children here.
We beg You, grant what they propose –
To celebrate her eightieth year!

Notes

PN 2

20 February 1894

This date was both Mère Gonzague's birthday and the first anniversary of the day on which she became Novice Mistress at the end of a term as Prioress.

St. 5, l. 1 'Rose': the allusion is to the recipient's Christian name, Rosalie.

4. SAINT CECILIA

All the time the instruments were playing,
Cecilia was singing in her heart . . .
(Office of the Church)

O Saint I love so much, ' with joy I contemplate
That shining track-of-light ' that stays here after you.
I think I'm hearing still ' your melody! . . . ah, straight
From Heav'n your harmonies ' come down to me
    anew.
I'm still in exile, so ' to you my prayers are raised:
Oh, let me take my rest ' on your pure heart. For here
That spotless lily shone ' – on earth its splendour
    blazed:
So marvellous a flower ' had hardly any peer.

9 When suitors called, not one, ' Chaste Dove, did you
    admit –
For Jesus was the Love ' that you were wedded to:
He chose your soul, and to ' Himself united it;
Such virtues did He find ' – such fragrances in you! . . .
One mortal – youth ashine – ' he, too (to your
    distress)
Had breathed your perfume in, ' O heav'nly flower of
    white;
He sought to gather you ' – to gain your tenderness:
Valerian, who brought ' his heart, with love alight.
And, soon, he had prepared ' a sumptuous wedding
    feast
And singers through the halls ' of all his palace sang:
Yet, in your maiden heart ' another song increased
Whose echo was divine ' and up to Heaven rang.

10

What *could* you sing – so far ' away your Home on
  high!–
In seeing, near to you, ' such mortal frailty?
Undoubtedly you wished, ' Cecilia, to die –
For Jesus, to be one ' with Him, eternally.
But no! I hear your lyre ' – angelic vibrances! –
The music of your love ' so sweetly it avows,
You raised up to the Lord ' that song whose words
  were this:
'Oh, keep me virgin-pure ' for You, my tender
  Spouse.'
Abandon (words here fail) ' – Divine the melody!
In that celestial hymn ' was love made manifest:
31 Such love as *does not fear*, ' forgets itself, to be
Upon the Heart of God ' a little child at rest . . .

So, to the vault of blue ' in purity there sailed
(To come and light it up) ' a white – a timid star . . .
Illumining the night, ' whose splendour was
  unveiled –
Thus, for this virgin pair, ' celestial glories are! . . .

Valerian dreamt, first, ' of earthly pleasure – for
Your love, Cecilia, ' was all that he desired –
And yet, in wedding you, ' discovered so much more;
In him, a love of Life ' Eternal you inspired!
'Young friend,' you said to him, ' 'near me – he
  never sleeps –
Here always, as a guard ' of my virginity,
An Angel of the Lord ' unending vigil keeps,
In joy, as with his wings ' of blue he covers me.
At night I see him – oh, ' his features then appear
More radiant than are ' the fires of dawn; for he
Is all a gentle flame: ' such purity is here,
The Face of God shines out ' of his transparency.'

Valerian replied, | 'This angel *show* to me,
And then I might believe | in what is sworn by you:
But tremble otherwise | – for, look at me, and see
The fury, and the hate | my love may turn into!'

O Dove inside the rock, | you're hidden there, you
    can
Be safe! you needn't dread | the hunter and his snare.
The Face of Jesus gives | you light. Valerian
Now reads your heart and finds | the Holy Gospel
    there . . .
Your answer came at once; | you smiled as you
    replied:
'Yes, you will see him, soon, | my Guardian! He'll
    come
To talk to you and tell | you all that will betide –
To soar to Heav'n you first | must face *your martyrdom.*
Before you see him, though, | your Baptism – you
    need
Your soul to be made white | by water; that is when
The True and Only God | will live in you indeed.
The Holy Spirit . . . He | will animate you then.
The Word – the Son of God, | the Son of Mary too –
With love that is immense | is on our altars here
As Sacrifice! The Bread | of Heav'n is offered you:
To banquet, thus, on Life, | Valerian, draw near!
The Seraph in the height | will call you 'brother' – for
He sees his God enthroned | in you, and will desire
To raise you from the shores | of earth, and he will
    draw
You up to where he dwells, | this ardency of fire.'
'My heart is now aflame: | a new felicity
(The nobleman exclaims) | has caught it and it soars!
The True and Only God | I want to live in me:
Cecilia! *my* love | will be no less than yours.'

12

When, afterwards, the Robe ' of Innocence he wore
Valerian could see ' the shining angel. Now
He gazed upon the strength ' and loveliness he saw,
Delighting in the rays ' from that angelic brow.
The Seraph, as he shone ' held roses, and their red
Had, in them, interlaced, ' a lily-burst of white.
(These blossoms opened up ' in Heaven's flower-bed,
Beneath the rays of Love ' of God's creative Light.)

'Dear heav'nly spouses! Crowns ' of Roses, soon,
　　will ring
Your brows,' the Angel said; ' 'There are no words
　　for this –
No voice, nor any lyre ' whose cadences can sing
Of martyrdom – of how ' immense a grace it is!
I cannot suffer so ' – though we, the Seraphim,
Are plunged in the abyss ' of God's own Beauty, I
Can never give Him tears, ' nor give, as you to Him
My blood; despite my love ' – for, oh! I cannot die.
Though *we* have purity ' as our angelic lot
(Our joy will never end) ' – though that is wholly
　　true,
Compared with us, a great ' advantage you have got:
96 For you can both be pure ' and suffer for Him too.
. . . . . .

'Virginity's the state ' these lilies symbolize
(Sweet gift they, from the Lamb) ' . . . so fragrant
　　will you be!
An aureole of white ' your glory signifies –
A song that's wholly new ' you'll sing, eternally!
Your union, so chaste, ' yet many souls will bear
Who Him as their true love, ' Him only, have
　　professed:
You'll see them shine in Heav'n ' like flames of
　　loving there,

13

Before the throne of God, | the heart-home of the
  Blest.'

Lend me, Cecilia! | your melody. Anew
I'd make a crowd of hearts | love Jesus as they should;
Would immolate my life | completely, as did you,
Would offer Him as gifts | my weeping and my blood.
Obtain for me the taste | of perfect sacrifice –
Abandon – Fruit of Love | upon this foreign shore.
Obtain for me, dear Saint, | that, soon, my soul may
  rise
To Heaven, where I'll be | near you, for evermore.

Notes

PN 3

28 April 1894 (Céline's twenty-fifth birthday)

' . . . alas, it would need another tongue than that of earth to
express the beauty of the *abandon* [self-surrender] of a soul in the
hands of Jesus . . . *Céline*, the story of *Cecilia* (*the Saint of*
ABANDON) is your story too!' (Letter from Thérèse, 26 April
1894).

Thérèse wrote this poem for her sister, Céline, then looking after
their sick father. With her thoughts on the future, she wanted to
direct Céline's mind towards consecrated virginity, 'fruitful loss'
as she called it in Poem 26. (But Thérèse said of her parents,
whose holiness flowered in matrimony: 'God gave me a mother
and father more worthy of heaven than of earth.')

Cecilia is an historical figure, a Roman martyr, probably of the
late second/early third century. But the *Acts of the Martyrdom of St
Cecilia*, which gives the legend on which Thérèse based her poem,
is a 'pious romance' of the fifth century.

Abandon I have left untranslated this French word (it should be pronounced as in English). Neither 'surrender' (my first translation of it) nor 'abandonment' will quite do. See page xxi for an indication of its meaning. As used by Thérèse, it has overtones of the utter trust of a child in the arms of its loving parent.

ll. 9–10 Lit. 'In going through life, you never sought any other spouse but Jesus'.

ll. 31–32 are key lines on *abandon*.

l. 36 Lit. 'The virginal love of the spouses in Heaven.'

l. 96 The dots between this and the next line come from Thérèse (seemingly to indicate transition to a different idea). Nothing has been omitted.

5. HYMN TO OBTAIN THE CANONIZATION OF THE VENERABLE JOAN OF ARC

1   O God of hosts, the Church – the whole of us
Would like, upon the Altar soon, to sing
Of Maid, of Martyr; she the Valorous!
Her praises through the courts of Heaven ring.

Refrain 1
O King! Advance
Your Maid's renown:
And give to Joan of France
The Altar and the Crown!

2   To conquer? No: to save the guilty France
(None other could have); *that* she battled for.
Let heroes – all, together! – take their stance,
But still a martyr (such as she) weighs more.

3   For Joan is simply, Lord, Your work of art –
What on this timid Maid did You endow?
A warrior's soul You gave – a burning heart;
You wished to place Your laurels on her brow.

4   Joan in a field heard Voices call from Heav'n,
They summoned her to fight! Ah, what a wild
Commission – *saving France* – she had been giv'n.
The army was commanded by this Child!

5   She won the souls of haughty fighting-men –
How pure the gaze of her, the Heaven-sent!
She captured them with words of flame; and then
Before her were the boldest foreheads bent.

6   A marvel, this – unique in history:
    One sees a king who trembled with alarm
    And yet won back his crown . . . how can this be?
    He did it through a feeble child's right arm!

7   It is not, though, the victories of Joan
    That we desire today to celebrate.
    For, Lord, her *true* renown to us is known:
    Her virtues shone abroad, her love was great.

8   Yes, Joan saved France, she led a holy war:
    But what had then her virtues to arouse?
    A seal of bitter suffering she bore,
    The blessed stamp of Jesus as her Spouse.

9   Joan gave up life – a high oblation, and
    Heard singing at the stake: because the Blest
    Drew up this exile to her Native Land –
    Again this Saving Angel was at rest.

10 O Joan – for you our only hope remain –
    We beg you, hear us: from the height sublime
    Come down to us, convert our France again –
    Yes, come and save her for a second time!

        Refrain 2
        May God advance
        His arms! Our plea
        Is that you'll save our France
        Again, and make her free.

11 Daughter of God of Battles! ah, how tall
    You were, in chasing out the Englishmen!
    Remember, though, the days when you were small:
    For feeble lambs were all you guarded then.

Refrain 3
Your warrior's arts
Use in defence,
Today, of children's hearts,
And of their innocence.

12   Sweet Martyr, you have *us*: the convent doors
Enclose your sisters, Joan. What is our rôle,
The object of our prayer? The same as yours –
We pray that God may reign in ev'ry soul.

Refrain 4
Give us – as seal
On our desire –
An apostolic zeal,
O Joan! your Martyr's-fire.

13   Away from ev'ry heart will fear have flown
When we shall see the Church, our Mother, bring
The Saintly Crown to wreathe our lovely Joan –
Then will it be that all of us can sing:

Refrain 5
Our hopes today
Are in your hands.
Then pray for us – O pray
For us, Saint Joan of France!

Notes

PN 4

8 May 1894

The above date, which Thérèse wrote on the manuscript of her poem, was a day of special celebration in Lisieux, as throughout France. Earlier that year Pope Leo XIII had authorized the introduction of the Cause of Beatification of Joan of Arc, thus according Joan the title 'Venerable' and permitting her to be honoured and prayed to publicly.

Pierre Cauchon, closely involved in the condemnation of Joan when Bishop of Beauvais, afterwards became Bishop of Lisieux. A later Bishop, Thomas Basin, was one of the promoters of Joan's rehabilitation in 1455–56.

On 8 May 1894, five thousand people crowded into the Cathedral of St Pierre at Lisieux. A 'rich standard of the glorious Liberatress' was placed in the chapel containing Cauchon's tomb. Céline, with other young people preparing for the occasion, had made 'twelve large white oriflammes scattered with fleurs-de-lys'.

St. 11, l. 1 'how tall'. Thérèse wrote 'How beautiful were your steps', a phrase taken from Song of Songs 7:1.

Refrain 4, literally, refers to a desire to 'save souls'.

6. MY SONG OF TODAY

1   My life's a jot of time,
>   an hour that comes and goes;
My life – a day, not more –
>   escapes and runs away.
To give You while on earth,
>   O God, the love one owes,
I've got ... only today!

2   I love you, Jesus; *You*
>   this soul aspires to! I
Wish – only for today –
>   my head on You to lay:
Come, rule my heart, and smile
>   upon me in reply –
This, but just for today!

3   What do I care, O Lord,
>   that darkness may pervade?
Tomorrow – ah, for that
>   I simply cannot pray! ...
Oh make my heart stay pure,
>   enwrap me in Your shade:
This, but just for today.

4   Tomorrow? Dream of that
>   and wavering I fear –
I worry and am sad
>   at trouble on its way:
But trials here I want,
>   O God, and suff'ring here;
These I want, for today.

5   I *shall* behold You soon
                        on that eternal shore,
      O God, my Pilot! where
                        I shall my anchor weigh:
      My little boat, in peace,
                        guide through the thunder-roar:
         This, but just for today.

6   Lord, let me hide myself –
                        find refuge in your Face,
      No longer hear the world
                        and all its idle bray.
      Ah, give to me your love
                        and keep me in your grace –
         This, but just for today.

7   The nearness of your Heart
                        forgetfulness ensures:
      No longer to the fears
                        of night am I a prey.
      O Jesus, grant a place
                        inside that Heart of yours:
         This, but just for today.

8   O sacred Mystery!
                        O Bread of Heaven's height!
      O Living Bread, of Love's
                        bestowal! come, I pray –
      Come, Jesus; live within
                        my heart, O Host of white –
         This, but just for today.

9   O deign that You, the Vine
                    I'll stay united to:
      For You, this feeble branch
                    will all its fruit display;
      Then, harvest-grapes of gold
                    I can be off'ring You,
      Lord . . . from when? From today!

10   This harvest-gift of love –
                    with souls for grapes – must be
      Made up in just a day,
                    this day that flies away:
      A true Apostle's fire,
                    O Jesus, give to me! –
      This, but just for today.

11   O Spotless Virgin, you're
                    the star by which I sail.
      You give me Jesus; you
                    unite me with Him. May
      I rest, O Mother, in
                    the safety of your veil:
      This, but just for today.

12   My Guardian Angel, come
                    enfold me in your wing,
      Behold me, where I am –
                    light up for me the way.
      I call on you for help,
                    direct my journeying!
      This, but just for today.

13   I want to see You, Lord
                    unveiled, uncloudedly;
      But, far from You I pine,
                    in exile. So I say:
      'Oh, that You will not hide
                    your lovely Face from me!' –
      This, but just for today.

14   I soon shall fly to You,
                    to praise You, my Desire.
      When day without an end
                    sheds on my soul its ray,
      I shall be singing – to
                    the Holy Angels' lyre –
      That Eternal 'Today'!

Notes

PN 5

1 June 1894, Feast of the Sacred Heart of Jesus

'We have only the brief instant of life to give to the good God . . .
and already He is preparing to say, "Now it's my turn . . ."'
(Thérèse, letter to Céline, 19 August 1894).

This poem was written as a feast-day gift for her sister, Marie
(Sister Marie of the Sacred Heart).

Metre the first syllable of each last line should be heavily stressed.
This reproduces a first syllable of intensity in the French.

St. 2, l. 2 Lit. (addressed to Jesus): 'For one day only, stay (as)
my gentle support.'

St. 4, l. 1 'wavering', i.e. inconstancy.

St. 7, l. 1 forgetfulness, literally, 'of everything that passes'.

7. THE PORTRAIT OF A SOUL I LOVE

*Written for her sister, Marie. An acrostic, the initial
letters of the lines spelling 'Marie du Sacré Cœur'.*

My portrait's of a heart ' I know, a loving soul;
A faith received from Heav'n, ' a high and soaring thing:
Responsive to no joy ' on earth, her only goal
Is Jesus. Him she names, ' in ardency, her King.
Exactly does one say ' she's generous and great;

Does not that humble heart ' – so lively – set its sight
Upon the shining star, ' the far horizon, straight? –

So often thus her soul ' will with her Lord unite!
At one time she'd a love ' of independence: she'd
Chase happiness – pure, this – ' and freedom true.
    To spill
Real benefis around ' was this one's joyous need:
Effacement of herself ' – that, only, was her will.

Caught up, and captured by ' His heart, this soul became
O'Er-come by Love! – the work ' of His creative Art;
Until . . . I'll see her there, ' pure-burning, like a flame,
Resplendent up in Heav'n, ' close to the Sacred Heart.

Notes

PN 6

1 June 1894

This acrostic in verse would have accompanied Poem 6 as a feast-day gift to Marie du Sacré Cœur (Marie of the Sacred Heart).

It was Marie, Thérèse's eldest sister and godmother, who prepared her for First Communion: 'I sat on her knee and listened *avidly* to what she told me. She spoke of the immortal riches that it is easy to amass every day, and of what a misfortune it is to pass by without wanting to make the effort to stretch out one's hand to take them: and then she showed me the way in which one can become *holy* through fidelity in little things . . .' (*Aut*, Ms.A).

8. SONG OF THANKS TO OUR LADY OF MOUNT CARMEL

Written for, and in the person of, Sister Martha of Jesus

1   Dear Mother, when my life began
Your arms enclosed me: they would be
Around me constantly – I can
Say 'Always they protected me!'
For innocence' sake, you placed
Me in the sweetest nest! – its span,
A holy cloister's shade, was spaced
To guard my childhood by your plan.

2   Then later, that I might say 'yes'
To Jesus (for my youth was when
I heard His call) . . . in tenderness
You came and showed me Carmel then.
'Ah, come, my child – be generous'
(You spoke so gently to me) 'vow –
Near me you will be happy thus –
Give your self for your Saviour now.'

3   My tender Mother, near to you –
Ah, what repose of heart I've known!
On earth this can't be added to:
My joy is Jesus – Him alone.
If sometimes I am sad or I'm
A prey to fear attacking me,
Your blessing, Mother, every time,
Shores up my own infirmity.

4   Oh, grant that, faithful still and strong
In Jesus – God, my Bridegroom – I
One day, up to the Heav'nly throng
In answer to His call, shall fly!
Then – suff'ring but a thing that's been,
My exile over – I'll prolong
My thanks: for this, to Carmel's Queen
The Lovable, shall be my song.

Notes

PN 7

16 July 1894, Feast of Our Lady of Mount Carmel

July 16, besides being the great feast of the Carmelite Order, was the birthday of Sister Martha of Jesus (Florence Cauvin), a lay-sister and one of the novices instructed by Thérèse.

Sister Martha said to the beatification tribunal: 'I inflicted a great deal of suffering on (Thérèse) through my difficult temperament.' Her testimony needs to be read as a whole, so simple, vivid and moving a document is it. She underwent a spiritual transformation, it is recorded, before she died in 1916.

St. 1, l. 6 'the sweetest nest'. Florence, having lost her mother when she was six, was brought up by the Sisters of St Vincent de Paul. Hence Thérèse's reference to 'a holy cloister'.

9. PRAYER OF THE CHILD OF A SAINT

1   Recall that here on earth your happiness
Lay in your looking after us! We pray
That you who go on loving us, will bless
Your children – will protect us still today.
You've reached your Homeland, where
             you're met and greeted by
Our mother dear – there, long
          before you, up on high:
In Heaven now you reign
Together. Both again,
        Watch over us!

2   Recall Marie, that darling daughter who,
Your eldest, was the dearest to you ... yes,
Recall, as well: she made life full for you
With all her love and charm and happiness.
God called her then, so – for
          His sake – you didn't cling:
Instead, you blessed the hand
         that offered Suffering.
Your lovely 'Diamond' – oh,
The one that sparkled so,
        Remember now!

3   And Pauline – she the 'Pearl of Beauty' – too:
At home, a weak and timid 'lamb' – but how
God's strength has since possessed the one you
    knew;
It's she who leads the flock of Carmel now.

Yes, she is Mother to
                your other children here –
Papa! come guide that one
                to you so very dear!
            Still, from your place above,
            Your little Carmel love! . . .
                Remember now . . .

4   Your *third* child now recall, and all the prayer
        You offered up to God, so ardently . . .
        He heard! Like, here below, her sisters there
        She's splendid as a lily, Léonie.
    The Visitation hides
                her from the world, but she
    Loves Jesus; and His peace
                now floods her like a sea.
            Recall, and hear the sighs –
            Her ardent longings – rise,
                Remember now!

5   Recall, now, your dear Céline also: she
        The angel who was taking care of you
        (For then God's gaze had meant that you would be
        Tried, by a choice so glorious – there too).
    You reign in Heav'n . . . her task
                is finished. By her vow
    Her life is given up
                to Jesus wholly now.
            Protect her, we entreat,
            The one you hear repeat,
                'Recall me now!'.

6   Remember, too, your 'Little Queen': *you* know –
      The 'Orphan of the River', as we say!
      Recall: her little footsteps faltered so,
      Your guiding hand it was that showed the way
     Papa, you wished your child
              to keep her childhood: hence
    You sought (for God alone)
              to guard her innocence . . .
          Her locks of gold – a sight
          That gave you such delight –
             Recall them now!

7   And always, too, up in the belvedere
      You'd take her on your knee, and you would bring
      Contentment to her with a prayer . . . she'd hear
      The gentle cradle-song that you would sing.
    What she would see was Heav'n
             reflected in your face
   When, there, your gaze was drawn
            profoundly into space.
          Songs . . . of *Eternity*:
          The Beauty there would be!–
             Recall that now.

8   One Sunday – how that day was full of light –
      You pressed her to your heart, a father . . . you,
      In giving her a little flower of white,
      Agreed that *she* could fly to Carmel too!
    Papa! your love throughout
              her heavy trials here
   Gave ev'ry proof to her
            that it was most sincere.
         At Bayeux, and at Rome,
         You showed her Heav'n – her Home!–
            Recall that now.

9   Recall we saw the Holy Father's hand
       Rest on your forehead. Yet there was concealed
       One mystery! ... you couldn't understand
       The print of God by which your brow was sealed.
    Your children bless the cross,
                   your bitter sorrow – how
    You suffered then! But they
                   are praying to you now.
          Your forehead bears a sign,
          In Heav'n! ... in rays that shine,
              Nine lilies flower!!!

Notes

PN 8

August 1894

'... the holy patriarch who has delighted Heaven by his fidelity' (Thérèse, letter to Céline, 6 July 1893).

Thérèse's father, Louis Martin, died on 29 July 1894. He had suffered, from 1887 onwards, a series of strokes, which had been followed by some disorder of mind. The death of Louis meant that it would now be possible for Céline to enter Carmel, if a fourth Martin sister were accepted there.

From Thérèse's knowledge of Louis' holiness – and because an event which she audaciously told God would be a sign from Heaven immediately took place – Thérèse was certain that Louis had gone straight to God: hence the title of the poem.

Louis, and his wife Zélie, Thérèse's mother (d. 1877), were declared 'Venerable' on 26 March 1994: a step in their joint beatification cause.

St. 2, l. 7 'Diamond': Louis' pet name for Marie.

St. 3, ll. 1–2 'Pearl of Beauty' / 'lamb': 'Real pearl' (*perle fine*) and 'lamb' were Louis' pet names for Pauline.

St. 4, l. 5 'The Visitation': the Visitation Convent at Caen.

St. 5, ll. 3–4 'glorious choice', i.e. choice by God, in relation to Louis' suffering. In *Aut.* (Ms. A) Thérèse, in referring to her father's illness, describes it as a 'glorious trial'.

St. 6, l. 1 'Little Queen': Louis' pet name for Thérèse herself, much quoted by Thérèse (*Aut.*, Ms. A) in describing her life at Les Buissonnets, the family home in Lisieux.

l. 2 'Orphan of the River'. The French is 'L'orpheline de la Bérésina', another of Louis' pet names for Thérèse; perhaps comparable to the English 'orphan of the storm'. The Beresina, a river in White Russia, was the scene of a disaster during the retreat from Moscow in 1812. A novel called *L'orpheline de Moscou, ou la jeune institutrice* by Mme Noilliez was at Les Buissonnets, Thérèse's childhood home in Lisieux.

St. 9, l. 9 'Nine lilies' A little after her father's death, Thérèse made and decorated a chasuble from a gown of her mother's. The design, within a cross, was of the Holy Face together with two white roses (her parents), four lily buds (her brothers and sisters who died in infancy) and five lilies (her sisters and herself).

10. PRAYER OF A CHILD IN EXILE

Written for her sister Marie to send to Father Almire Pichon.
Another acrostic, the initial letters spelling 'Almire'.

A well-loved Priest I know, ' I now am praying for.
Love drove him, Lord, to preach ' Your Sacred Heart to
all.
My thoughts are with him – still ' upon that foreign
shore;
I beg – it's time! – in *France* ' Your shepherd to instal.
Return their guide and light, ' Your children now
implore:
Evangelize us, here! ' This Father, Lord, recall.

Notes

PN 9

11 September 1894

Father Almire Pichon, a Jesuit, was spiritual director of Thérèse's
sister, Marie. The latter asked Thérèse to write a poem for the
feast day of his name-saint. He was then a missionary in Canada.
On the occasion of Marie's Profession in 1888, Thérèse herself
made to him a general confession that was important to her.

11. THE STORY OF A SHEPHERDESS BECOME QUEEN

Written for the Profession Day
of Sister Marie-Madeleine

1   We've come to sing, O Madeleine,
This lovely day you make your vows,
About the marvel of that chain
Which gently binds you to your Spouse.
Hear now the charming story: Once
A shepherdess became the choice,
The loved one, of a King! . . . she runs
Toward him when she hears his voice.

Refrain
This shepherdess sing:
Since Heaven's High King –
She, here, being poor –
Will marry her! – now, evermore.

2   Look at this little shepherd-girl –
She guards her lambs, and spins, as she
Sees how the flower-buds unfurl,
Delights in birdsong from the tree;
Attuned to what all things declare
In those great woods and that blue sky . . .
For everything of beauty there
Revealed to her her God on high.

3   She loving *them* so ardently,
Jesus and Mary, to impart
Proof of their love for Mélanie,
Talked to her one day, heart to heart.

34

'Will you,' the Gentle Queen invites,
'Live near me, and for name be giv'n
"Madeleine"? There, on Carmel's heights,
You will gain nothing else than *Heav'n*!

4   'Child, leave here, with light heart, and count
Your flock no longer: now I am
Calling you to my sacred mount,
Jesus will be your only Lamb.'
'Oh! come, your soul has captured me,'
Repeated Jesus, 'for I vow
I take you for my bride-to-be,
You will be mine for ever, now!'

5   Hearing, the shepherdess at once
In joy, sets out and will not stop;
Helped by her Mother, Mary – runs
And climbs Mount Carmel to the top.
. . . . . .
It's you, O Madeleine, we mean!
Of *you*, on this great day, we sing:
A Shepherdess become a Queen,
Jesus, your love – He is your King.

6   My dearest Sister, this you know:
To serve our God – *that* is to reign!
The Gentle Saviour, here below,
Throughout his teaching made this plain:
'Your aim is that in Heaven you
Shall have all other souls surpassed?
Then *this*, life-long, you'll have to do –
Hide yourself, wholly . . . be the last.'

7   O happy Madeleine! you're at
Your place in Carmel, where your prayer
To Jesus . . . *could* one toil in that,

Being so close to Heaven there?
Martha and Mary both! – for you
Pray to and serve your Saviour – yes,
This end you always have in view;
It gives you your true happiness.

8   If sometimes bitter suffering
Has come to you, to be a guest
Make it your joy, that bitter thing –
Suff'ring for God is sweet and blest.
Divine caresses thereupon
Will make you, soon, forget you tread
Those jagged thorns you're walking on –
You'll think you're flying then, instead!

9   The Angels envy you, and they,
Seeing your happiness, are awed
At that which you possess today –
Being the spouse, now, of the Lord!
Ah, yes! that King the saints adore
Has chosen you as spouse and bride:
Here, even, Marie! Evermore
You'll reign with Jesus, at His side.

Refrain
Soon will – Heav'n her gain –
The shepherdess reign
(She, here, being poor)
By the side of God, evermore!

To our Reverend Mothers:
10   O good and tender Mothers, who
Helped Madeleine, our Sister there –
Her peace and happiness are due
To your solicitude and prayer.

36

She'll know how to be grateful for
Your tender and maternal love:
Her God and Master evermore
Will lavish joys on you, above!

Last refrain:
Good Mothers – a sign
In your crowns that shine,
Will this flower appear . . .
That you offer our Saviour here!

Notes

PN 10

20 November 1894

'. . . behold, thy time was the time of lovers: and I spread my garment over thee . . . saith the Lord God: and thou becamest mine . . . I clothed thee with embroidery . . . and put . . . a chain about thy neck . . . thou . . . wast made exceeding beautiful: and wast advanced to be a queen' (Ezekiel 16: 8–13), quoted by Thérèse in Ms. A: 'God accomplished for me what Ezekiel reports in his prophecies'.

Sister Marie-Madeleine (Mélanie Lebon), a lay sister strikingly handsome of feature, had been a shepherdess in actual fact. She herself wrote that as a novice she 'was not in a state to profit from' Thérèse's advice, 'but after (Thérèse's) entry into heaven, I surrendered to her the care of my soul, and how she changed me! It's unbelievable! . . . I don't recognize myself any more.' Her testimony to the diocesan tribunal is frank and moving.

St. 5 The dots are Thérèse's; nothing has been omitted.

12. IT'S GONE AT LAST, THE TIME OF TEARS

*The first of two poems written for the ceremony of the reception
of the Carmelite habit by Sister Marie-Agnès of the Holy
Face, later called Marie of the Trinity. She had been
clothed as a Carmelite before, in Paris.*

1   Despite my helplessness, I want to sing,
O Virgin Mary, on this lovely day
An ev'ning hymn of thanks . . . My hope I bring –
That I be His, and wholly made away!
So distant from the holy ark, for long
My poor heart kept the thought of Carmel dear:
And now I've found it, and, my courage strong,
I've come, to taste the start of Heaven here.

Refrain
For now it's gone at last, the time of tears –
With fleece like all the flock I am consoled:
Ahead, a new horizon I behold
As, Mother, this enchanting day appears.
Hide me! This feeble lamb you hold,
In your Mantle fold.

2   Although I'm very young, yet suffering
Has come, its bitter trials to impart:
O Mary, you're the hope of whom I sing,
It's you who make your lamb so glad of heart.
You give me Carmel for my family!
A little child of yours, their sister – both.
Dear Mother, I will now your daughter be;
My Saviour, Jesus – He has now my troth.

3   Your Son has – though the words to say it fail –
Looked down, and has my feeble soul descried:
I've sought His holy Features – they avail
To draw me up, to Him in whom I'll hide.
What's necessary now is staying small,
To merit thus the gazing of His eyes.
My virtues will grow bigger, though – but all
Beneath that Ardent Beacon of the skies!

4   Kind Mary, I am not afraid of work –
Good will at least I have, and that you know.
I've faults, and yet I've courage not to shirk:
The charity is great my sisters show.
As I await my lovely wedding day
Their virtues I will reproduce in me;
I feel you giving strength, and so I say:
'The spouse of Jesus – that is what I'll be.'

Last Refrain
I ask you: bless those Reverend Mothers who,
In goodness, made my way to Carmel plain;
May each to an eternal throne attain;
O Mother, may I see them near to you.
    For each – O Virgin Mary, deign –
      A Crown to obtain.

Notes

PN 11

18 December 1894

'What's necessary now is staying small' goes to the very heart of Thérèse's spirituality.

'"Lord," replied St Peter, "we have fished all night and have caught *nothing*." Perhaps if he had caught some *little fishes* Jesus would not have worked a miracle, but he had *nothing* so Jesus soon filled his net in a way that almost made it break. Mark well the *character* of Jesus. He gives as God, but He wants *humility* of *heart*.' (Thérèse, letter to Céline, 26 April 1894).

13. BEFORE YOU, VIRGIN M*

1   Before you, Virgin Mary, we
       Are singing . . . What we've come to do
       Is pray for this dear child; and she
       Has put her hope in none but you.

2   You've waited for this day – oh, how
       You lift her, such a joy you rouse!
       Her tent set up on Carmel, now
       She only waits for Holy Vows.

3   What this reminds her of is when
       O tender Mary! earlier
       A joyful day was hers: for then
       Your mantle came to cover her.

4   At last, the homespun's done its task
       This second time it's giv'n by you.
       May she be habited, we ask
       By double of your spirit too.

5   'I've courage, so I will not shirk',
       She sang. 'That's true!' we thought inside,
       She also sang 'I like to work':
       Well, work – in plenty – we'll provide!

6   But strength is such a splendid thing
       For working with a zeal-that-glows:
       So, to her cheeks O Mother, bring
       The brilliant colour of a rose.

7 For her the waiting's over! Clothed,
  She'll taste, at last, a peace sublime
  As Jesus, seeing his betrothed,
  Comes down to her at Christmastime.

8 Then, may He hide her in His Face –
  This lamblet, tender Mother! At
  That permanence she seeks a place;
  She wants no resting-bower but that.

9 Your feeble lamb – O Mary, say
  She will (her wishes met) be found
  Safe-hidden through life's night: oh, may
  Your mantle's folds wrap her around.

10 May your Maternal heart, we pray,
  Long guard her Mothers here: they were
  The ones whose loving gives, today,
  Her cherished Carmel back to her.

Notes

PN 12

18 December 1894

The preceding poem, No.12, is written in the persona of the Sister herself. The present poem looks at the same Clothing ceremony through the eyes of the community into which she is being received.

A word about Sister Marie of the Trinity (Marie-Louise Castel). Her puckish face is easily distinguishable in photographs of the community. She had left the Paris Carmel through ill-health, and seemed to lack emotional stability when she became a novice in Lisieux. Thérèse showed her great affection and recognized her generosity of spirit. She steadied her. This nun's testimony to the diocesan and apostolic tribunals shows admirable maturity.

St. 4, 1. 1 'the homespun': French 'la bure', the brown Carmelite habit.

St. 10, 1. 1 'we pray' The French expands on this; the Community prays for a granting of the prayers of the newly-clothed nun, as well as for the Reverend Mothers who brought her to Carmel.

14. THE QUEEN OF HEAVEN, TO HER BELOVED CHILD, MARIE

'Marie of the Holy Face' was the name as a postulant of Thérèse's sister, Céline. She later became Sister Geneviève.

1   A little child I'm seeking, who's
    Like Jesus . . . this I want to do –
    To guard her, with my Lamb: I'll use
    Only one cradle for the two.

2   In heaven's Angels, jealousy
    Your happy lot might well arouse!
    I'll nonetheless give you, Marie,
    The Holy Child to be your Spouse . . .

3   I sought a child I wished to be
    Jesus's sister . . . *you* I chose.
    Will you, then, keep Him company?
    My heart is here for your repose.

4   I'll hide and cradle you (this veil
    Shelters the King of Heaven too):
    My glorious Son will never fail
    To be the bright daystar for you.

5   But, shelter always? That you may
    Under my veil with Jesus hide,
    A little one you'll have to stay,
    By childhood virtues beautified.

6   Thought wanting you to radiate
      Both gentleness and purity,
      What most I give, to animate
      Your spirit, is simplicity.

7   The great God – One, in Persons three;
      The angels tremble at His power,
      Eternal One! – wants here to be
      No grander than a meadow-flower.

8   The simple daisy, open-eyed,
      Looks upward on its slender stem:
      You be a sister-flower beside
      The little Babe of Bethlehem!

9   His charms – a King in exile, He –
      The world, though, fails to recognize:
      And, often, tears of grief you'll see
      Glistening in his baby eyes.

10   Forget (you must!) your weariness,
      To make this lovely Child rejoice:
      Your chains – so gentle! – you should bless,
      Gently and with a lilting voice.

11   Great God, who causes billows wild
      To hush – what did You come to seek?
      To make Yourself a little child! –
      For us, becoming small and weak.

12   The Uncreated Word, to be
      Your little Brother! and my Son!
      An exile here . . . for you, Marie:
      What words now will He utter? None!

13   Let this be His first token and
Unutterable love convey.
God's *silent* speech you'll understand,
You'll imitate it every day.

14   If sometimes Jesus sleeps, you will
Stay in repose, beside Him, too! –
His Heart (at watch, though He is still)
Will gently be supporting you.

15   The work's no worry, dear Marie,
For what your daily labour tells
Is how you love (and that should be
Your work – *all love*, and nothing else).

16   If someone comes along and says
'What is there from your work to show?',
'I love, and much, so I possess'
You say, 'such *riches*, here below!'

17   With bays will Jesus wreathe your brow
If you want nothing but His love:
If you're abandoned to Him now,
You'll reign forever, up above.

18   You'll see Him gaze at you – the night
Will be ablaze that once was black!
You'll fly to Heav'n, in high delight,
With nothing now to hold you back!

Notes

PN 13

25 December 1894, a Christmas gift to Céline, placed in her shoe.

'Childhood, which in natural life is only a transitory state leading to adulthood, becomes, in the sphere of grace, the ideal state, the final flowering of the whole spiritual destiny. The Christian will no longer strive to pass beyond this new childhood but to tend toward it . . .' (Père Victor de la Vièrge, OCD (Victor Sion), *Spiritual Realism of St Thérèse of Lisieux*.)

Early in the year which is about to begin, Thérèse's sister, Marie (Sister Marie of the Sacred Heart) will, by a simple question, cause Pauline (Mère Agnès) to order Thérèse to begin what became her autobiography: 'Is it possible that you should permit her to compose little poems to please everybody, and that she should write nothing for us about all the memories of her childhood?' (deposition to the diocesan tribunal).

15. THE ANGEL OF THE EUCHARIST

From 'The Angels at the Crib', Thérèse's play, in prose and verse, written for the nuns to perform at Christmas 1894.

The angels surrounding the crib in Bethlehem have their individual preoccupations as they cast their thoughts into the future: the Angel 'of the Resurrection', the Angel 'of the Last Judgement', and so on.

SCENE 4

The Angel of the Eucharist comes forward . . .

1   My brother angel, now see
The Lord up to Heaven go!
I am come down here, to be
At the altar bending low;
Where now, to the sight of all,
Almighty God, Who is hid –
Life's Author! – seems yet more small
Than as new-born child He did.

Refrain
Henceforth in this holy place –
Ah, from here I will not move!
My prayer to God I shall raise,
Shall offer my hymns of love;

2   My lyre His Beauty recite,
This hidden God! as I wait
Caught up in holy delight,
His charms that intoxicate.

If only I, too, could feed
On the God of Love each day!–
By a miracle indeed,
Unite with Him in that way.

Refrain
Oh, at least to souls in grace
I shall lend my ardour here!
That their Saviour in this place
They'll approach and have no fear.

Notes

RP 2 (extract)

Christmas, 1894.

St. 2. ll, 5–6: 'feed on the God of Love'. The French has, specifically, 'at the tabernacle'.

16. TO SAINT JOSEPH

1   Though poverty your life here knew,
        Saint Joseph, there is this to say:
        At Jesus, and at Mary you
        Gazed . . . upon *beauty* every day.

            Refrain
        Most tender Joseph, haste –
        Protect our Carmel! Oh,
        Let all your children, always, taste
        The peace of Heaven here below.

2   The Son of God, in infancy,
        How often by your arms was pressed,
        As, meek to your authority,
        He found upon your heart His rest.

3   Jesus and Mary . . . yes! we, too –
        In solitude we serve them: for
        We work to please them, as did you:
        That's what we want on earth – no more!

4   Our Mother, Saint Teresa – who
        Invoked your intercession, stressed
        That when, with love, she prayed to you
        You always answered her request.

5   And so . . . until our exile here
        Concludes, this joyous hope we share:
        In Heaven – with our Mother dear –
        Saint Joseph, we shall see you there!

Last refrain
We, tender Father, call!–
Our little Carmel bless:
Our exile over, may we all
Unite, in Heaven's happiness!

Notes

PN 14

1894

'I thank you, Monsieur l'Abbé, for having chosen me as godmother of the first child you will have the joy of baptizing; it is, then, up to me to choose the names of my future godchild. I want to give it as protectors: the Blessed Virgin, St Joseph, and St Maurice ...' (Thérèse, letter of 24 February 1897 to the Abbé Maurice Bellière).

St. 4, l. 1 'Our Mother, Saint Teresa': St Teresa of Avila.

St. 5, l. 3 In *this* stanza 'our Mother' refers to the Blessed Virgin.

17. THE ATOM OF THE SACRED HEART

Written at the request of Sister St Vincent de Paul, whose personal devotion it was to regard herself, in humility, as an 'atom'.

Refrain
Your atom, O Sacred Heart,
Here, her life outpoured,
Her joy and her peace, apart,
Is ... to charm you, Lord!

1   Your doorway I face
By night and by day,
And carried by grace –
Your Love – shout 'Hurray!'

2   Ciborium, where
God hides, out of sight ...
I want a nest there,
By day and by night.

3   With your wing, You make
For me, Jesus – see! –
A shelter ... I wake:
You're smiling at me.

4   You looked, and you came –
Ah, Jesus, my own!
Consume me with flame,
Like fire to the bone.

5   So tenderness-filled
        You speak and enthral.
        On your Heart I'm stilled,
        My Love and my All!

6   You soothe and support,
        With your Hand impart
        The courage you've taught
        The whimpering heart.

7   Whenever there's strain
        Bring heart-ease to me:
        As prodigal's gain
        The Good Shepherd be.

8   How wondrous! Behind
        The veil and the door,
        Where Love is enshrined,
        I stay, evermore.

9   Not earth is my good
        Or support: You send
        Your grace, in a flood –
        Ah, my only Friend!

10   Sweet martyrdom! I
        I am burning away
        O Jesus, I sigh
        For You, every day.

Notes

PN 15

1894

'Pray that the grain of sand [she herself] may become an ATOM perceptible only to the eyes of Jesus.' (Thérèse, letter to Pauline, 6 January 1889).

In the century in which Thérèse wrote, the image of the atom was one of extreme littleness. The French critical edition of the poems comments: 'Of course, they did not know at that time of the energy concealed in the atom – a discovery that would have enchanted the dynamic Thérèse.'

Sister St Vincent de Paul (Zoé Alaterre) was a lay-sister. Free with her comments, she saw Thérèse as a petit-bourgeois and kept goading her with comments like 'Come on, when are you going to start work?' Thérèse – who never shirked work, though she may not always have been adept at physical work – would have simply smiled back. Sister St Vincent was edifyingly recollected in her silent devotion before the Blessed Sacrament.

St. 1, l. 1 'doorway', i.e. the door of the tabernacle.

St. 4, l. 4 Like fire to the bone'. A free translation; Thérèse simply wrote *'sans retour'*, 'irrevocably'.

18. O HIDDEN GOD!

Written for the Epiphany

1   God, hid in childhood's features! yet to me
Clearly the King of Heav'n; I recognize
Your grandeur and Your mighty power. I see
Such gentle glory shining in Your eyes.
A thousand legions of Your angels would,
Called by You, come as Court from Heav'n above,
And strew Your crib with stars . . . make understood,
In song, that past all telling is Your Love.

R.1   This foreign shore surrounding You
(You cannot yet speak anything!) ...
My Saviour – God, and Brother too,
No gems, no sceptre Yours. I bring –
Adoring what's too deep to view –
Offer my gold, O God and King!

2   O King, You come, so lowly, from on high
To save the human race (Your brother!). I
Would like to suffer, for Your love ... I say
This, as You wish to die for me one day!
Of Your own Sorrow, offering a sign
(An aureole of Blood – I see it shine!),
I'd like to win You hearts O Jesus – here's
One gift to You to wipe away Your tears!

R.2   Receive the myrrh, O King who, by
Your Incarnation, wish to die.

Notes

PS 1

6 January 1895 or 1896

An unfinished poem, but the couplet with which it breaks off ('Receive the myrrh . . .') provides a striking and epigrammatic ending.

'THE ANGEL OF THE CHILD JESUS: Yes, the tears of Jesus are more sparkling than the splendours of Heaven . . . but what makes the height of my sorrow is thinking that this Child's gracious countenance will one day be hidden in a tomb . . . Then who will see him? . . . Who will be there to dry his tears? Mary herself will not be able to gaze upon the dear features of her adored Child!' (Thérèse's play, *The Angels at the Crib*, Christmas 1894).

19. JOAN'S HYMN AFTER HER VICTORIES

1   All, all! to You, Almighty, be
The glory of the battle-sword
(Since victory You gave to me –
A child so weak and timid, Lord.)
And oh, my Mother Mary! you,
A guiding planet, always bright –
Your lighting up my path, I knew,
Protected, from the Heavens' height.
When shall I go (from waiting here,
Sweet star whose gentle splendour shined!)
To see that blazing whiteness, clear? –
And, underneath your veil, to find
    Your heart a place of rest for me.

2   Earth's joys can not content my soul;
It wants Eternal Happiness!
It feels its exile here: its goal
Is God in Heav'n – and *nothing less.*
This, too, I want (before I go
To see my Jesus in His Light):
To win Him countless souls, and so
To love Him more and more. To fight!
And soon, on that celestial shore
(Life, here below, a single day),
He will embrace me, evermore!
The veiling cloud all rolled away,
    My Love, my Jesus, I shall see.

Notes

RP 3 (extract)

21 January 1895

'For my mission, like that of Joan of Arc, "the will of God will be accomplished in spite of the jealousy of men"' (Thérèse, on her death-bed, to Pauline).

St. 1. l. 4 'A child so weak ...' When Thérèse speaks of herself as little, it is not a childish complacency but an objective view of her relationship with God. If He is All, she is nothing without Him; nevertheless, she can do all things with His grace' (Père Victor de la Vièrge, OCD, op. cit.)

20. JOAN'S PRAYER IN PRISON

1   My Voices told of this: [|] in prison I am thrown –
I have no hope of aid, [|] except, O God, from You.
I left my father – and [|] he's old – for You alone:
I left the flowered fields, [|] the sky, unchanging
    blue.
For love of You alone [|] I left my vale. I came
And showed to those who fought [|] the standard
    of the Cross
As, Lord, the army I [|] commanded in Your name!
And generals – no less – [|] attended to my voice.

2   And now! – a prison cell, [|] the trophy that was due
For work and tears, and blood. [|] That recompense is
    mine!
I shall not see again [|] the places that I knew,
The smiling countryside [|] where meadow-flowers
    twine;
I shall not see again, [|] afar, the mountain-top –
Its snow, that mixed the blue [|] with white, as
    though a wave.
And never shall I hear [|] the chiming start and stop,
The bell which, in clear air, [|] its dreamy summons
    gave . . .

3   That star I seek in vain, [|] shut up in this dark jail,
Which sparkling in the sky [|] would ev'ning vigil
    keep,
I seek in vain the leaves [|] that served me as a veil
(I'd try to guard the flock [|] but then would fall
    asleep!).
When, now, between these tears, [|] my senses melt
    away

I dream about the vale, ' its charm of bush and tree,
The dew that comes at dawn, ' the scents of early day:
But then! . . . the clank of chains ' awakes me,
   suddenly.
   . . . . . .

4   My martyrdom! and I ' accept it, for Your love;
   No more do I fear death ' or dread the burning fire.
   For, Jesus, how my soul ' sighs now for You above –
   Aspires to You alone, ' my God and my Desire!
   I want to take my cross ' and follow You, to give
   My life for love of You, ' sweet Saviour. This is why
   I have one only wish. ' That I begin to live,
   That He and I be one, ' is why I want to die.

Notes

The dots between the third and fourth stanzas indicate omission
of prose and verse.

St. 1, l. 3 'for You alone': lit., 'for Your love alone'.

St. 2, l. 6 The image of a wave is one that I have added. It was
suggested by Pauline's substitution of *se plonge* for Thérèse's *se
mêle*, is mixed or mingled (the latter idea now restored to the
translation).

l. 7 'chiming start and stop'. Lit., an 'uncertain bell'.

21. JOAN'S VOICES DURING HER MARTYRDOM

1   From the Eternal Country we come down,
     To smile at you; you come to Heaven now:
     See, in our hands, your high immortal crown,
     To shine – a blaze of glory – on your brow.

2   Come with us, then, O Maid so dear,
        To radiant firmaments of blue;
        Come Home! No more your exile here! –
           Life, in our joyous sphere:
              God's daughter, you.

3   The stake is lit! God's Love, however – for
     It *also* is a Flame – it rises higher!
     Eternal Dew – ah! only minutes more –
     Will come to quench the torture of the fire.

4   Deliverance! The swaying bough,
        The martyr's palm, is waiting you:
        See (angel, liberator!) how
           Jesus comes to you now! –
              'Greatheart' and true.

5   Dear Martyr-Maid, a second and no more,
     Your suffering, and then eternal rest.
     Daughter of God, your death saves France! So draw
     Her children up, to live among the Blest.

Joan sings:

6   I enter Life, and, as I go,
     See saints and angels, there Above!
     I die to save my country so . . .
       Come to me, Mary – oh,
         Jesus, my Love!

Notes

The dots between the second and third stanzas indicate the omission of a short passage of prose.

St. 3, l. 3 'only minutes more'. Thérèse simply wrote 'soon', unspecifically. The 'second and no more' of a stanza coming later in her narrative (St. 5) reproduces Thérèse's specific '*un instant*' of suffering.

22. JOAN: THE DIVINE JUDGMENT

1   Dear sister who now calls,
                I answer you, my love:
       And now I break your bonds,
                unloosen ev'ry chain!
       Fly swiftly up to me,
                my fair and beauteous dove –
       For winter now is gone:
                in Heaven, *come and reign*!
         Yes, I your Judge decree it, Joan:
         Your Angel claims you as his own,
         And I – I make my judgment known:
      I've seen in you a burning flame of love.

2   So come, it is your Crowning-day,
         Beloved spouse, and I it is
         Who want to wipe your tears away.
         Oh, come to Me! receive my kiss.

3   To mountains above
            Companioned! Move
            Through meadows, my love,
              The Lamb drawing you:

4   O bride with my ring,
            This vale of the Spring
            Calls you. You shall sing
              Your song that is new . . .

5 They laud you, in Light,
The phalanx of white —
The Angels unite
 Melodiously.

6 Meek shepherdess, who
Are warrior, too —
Earth's honour of you
 Unended shall be.
Meek shepherdess, who
Are warrior — you
 Have *Heaven* from Me!

23. JOAN IN HEAVEN: THE CANTICLE OF TRIUMPH

The Saints address Joan:

1   This crown is yours, and for eternity:
This Martyr's-palm is yours:
        look also now on this –
The throne the Lord of Hosts
        has here prepared. For, see!
    Your throne it is.

2   Ah, in the Heavens here,
        pure singing-dove, remain –
For ever you've escaped
        the hunters and the snare.
You'll find the little brook
        that murmurs on the plain:
Wide meadows, and the flowers there.

3   Then, dove, take wing: on pinions of white,
Each high and golden star
        you can be visiting.
To Heav'n's aethereal vaults
        unending, rise in flight –
    O dove, take wing!

4   No enemies *now*, Joan! –
        No prison dark is yours.
The Seraph, as he shines,
        will call you sister fair.
See what your Love and Lord
        to you, His spouse, assures –
You, ever, on His Heart He'll bear.

Joan:

5   Ah, He is mine! . . . oh, joy beyond compare.
   All Heaven now is mine!

The Saints:
   All Heaven thine, we sing!

Joan:
All! Mary, angels, saints –
                  and God Himself! I'm heir
       To everything!

Note

St. 5 In the play the Saints three times echo Joan's 'mine!' with
their 'yours!'

24. PRAYER OF FRANCE TO JOAN OF ARC

France, personified, speaks:

1   Remember, Joan, the country of your birth –
The flower-coloured valleys, and recall
The fields that seemed exuberant with mirth.
To wipe away my tears, you left it all!
Remember also, Joan,
        that, angel-like and pure,
You saw your country's woes
        and came to bring the cure:
Your France, today – oh, hark! –
Is groaning in the dark:
        'Recall that now!'

2   And, Joan, recall the victories you'd win –
Orleans and then Reims would shower thanks.
Recall that you made glorious, and in
The name of God, the kingdom of the Franks.
But now, so far from you,
        I suffer and I sigh;
'Come, save me, once again,
        sweet martyr, Joan!', I cry.
Shear through these irons so.
The ills I've suffered – oh,
        Remember now.

. . . . . .

3   I come to you, and all in chains am bound,
A veil is hiding eyes that weepings mar:
In sorrows from my children I am drowned —
Not now among the greatest queens there are!
Forgotten, now, is God:
their Mother they neglect —
Your pity, to my woes —
so bitter, Joan! direct.
Console my heart! Advance
And save us! . . . for your France
Hopes in you now.

4   See, in my hands I hold my queenly crown —
Ah, Joan, I wish to place it on *your* brow:
Sweet sov'reign! it is you who must come down,
God's daughter, come and rule our people now.
See France's iron chains —
come break them, Joan! and then
'First Daughter of the Church'
may be our name again.
For Voices call — oh, hear!
A second time appear.
Come to us now.

Note

The dots between the second and third stanzas indicate a passage
in which Joan in heaven encourages France's approach to her.

68

25. SONG OF THANKS OF JESUS'S BETROTHED

Written for the day of Céline's clothing
in the habit of Carmel.

1   You've hidden me, for ever, in Your Face . . .
    My Jesus – God! Oh, hear me as I sing
    Of what is inexpressibly the grace
    Of having borne the Cross . . . of Suffering.

2   For long I've drunk a draught of tears, like You,
    I've shared Your cup of sorrows: yet in this
    That suffering has charms my heart knows too;
    One can save sinners – through the Cross, this is.

3   The Cross! by which my soul has grown in grace
    And light to see a new horizon by:
    Beneath the incandescence of Your Face
    My feeble heart, by You, is lifted high.

4   My Love, Your gentle voice is calling me;
    I hear Your 'Come, already Winter's gone!
    For you, my bride, the Spring begins to be.
    Night has at last its end. Behold the Sun!

5   'Lift up your eyes, and see your Homeland! Here
    You'll see – upon their thrones and honoured so –
    A well-loved Father and a Mother dear:
    Huge happiness like yours, to them you owe.

6   'Your life, a trice, will melt away, like dew –
      Heaven to Carmel's heights is very near:
      My loved one (for my Love has chosen you),
      I've kept a throne of glory for you here!'

Notes

PN 16

5 February 1895

'Let us not refuse Him the least sacrifice. Everything is so big in religion ... Picking up a pin through love can convert a soul! What a mystery!' (Thérèse, letter to Léonie, 22 May 1894).

26. LIVING BY LOVE!

1   In Love's last ev'ning-hours you would have heard
Jesus say plainly: 'He who would love Me,
Let him be true, let him obey my Word:
Father and Son his Visitants shall be.
Coming, to make his heart a dwelling-place,
We'll love him always! and Our Peace above
Shall fill him. For our will it is he stays
       In our own Love.'

2   Living by Love . . . means holding on to You
The uncreated Word, the Holy Name!
Jesus, I love You. You – God – know I do,
Love's Spirit sets me blazing with His flame.
My love of You attracts the Father – oh,
My feeble heart forbids Him to go free.
O Trinity – a Prisoner! as so
       Love-locked by me.

3   *To live* is by Your life and lovingly.
King, and the bright delight of Heaven's day,
Hidden as host of white You live for me:
Jesus, for You I'll also hide away!
Lovers must – night and day – have solitude,
The heart-to-heart which only it can give.
One glance from You gives me beatitude –
       By Love I live!

4   Living by Love . . . that means: don't pitch one's tent
On Thabor's summit when upon this earth,
But climb another hill where Jesus went;
Go with Him – know the Cross of priceless worth.
In Heav'n, I just must shout aloud and sing –
No trials as when love one had to prove!
In exile, this I want: in suffering
      Living by Love.

5   Living by Love means 'Give unendingly,
Claiming no earthly wage'. I do not doubt
This . . . I have stopped all counting up. I see
That when one loves, one doesn't measure out!
All to the heart of God (whose tenderness
Spills over!) I have given. And, that done,
Light – but my riches in me – on I press;
      Lovingly run.

6   Living by Love means banishing all fear –
All glancing-back to faults of earlier day:
Of my past sins I see no imprint here,
Love in a trice has burnt them all away.
O Fire Divine! O Furnace-flames' caress!
Here, in your hearth, I stay and will not move;
Singing within your fires in restfulness:
      'I live by Love! . . .'

7   Living by Love . . . 'Guard – in oneself, I mean –
One mighty Treasure in a mortal vase.'
Dear Love! I'm weak – as weak as ever seen;
I'm far from being an angel in the stars! . . .
But, if I fall in all the hours that go
You come and lift me up, and I receive
Grace, ev'ry passing second from You, so
      By Love I live.

72

8   Living by Love means 'Set unbroken course
     In spreading peace and joy to all in view.'
     Dear Pilot! Charity's my driving-force:
     In souls – my sisters – I am seeing You.
     Charity . . . *that's* the star that will not fail –
     On by its light and straight ahead I move.
     I've my device inscribed upon my sail:
         'Living by Love.'

9   Living by Love means too: while Jesus sleeps,
     Staying reposeful when rough waters roar.
     Don't fear I'll wake you up, Lord: on the deeps,
     Tranquil I wait to reach the Heav'nly shore . . . .
     Soon Faith will take and tear apart her veil,
     My Hope . . . it is to see You up on high.
     Charity swells and drives ahead my sail –
         By Love, live I!

10   Living by Love means . . . Master! to implore
     You spread Your Fires in priestly souls. For him,
     Your holy, sacred Priest – let him be more
     Pure in his spirit than the seraphim.
     Glory upon your Deathless Church confer,
     Do not be deaf, O Jesus, when I sigh.
     'Her child, I immolate myself for her:
         Love, I live by.'

11   Living by Love – the wiping of your Face,
     To win for sinners pardon of their sin –
     O God of Love, that they return to grace
     And bless your Name for ever – that to win!
     Blasphemy strikes my heart, I hear it still;
     To blot it out, I'll sing for evermore
     'Your name, your Sacred Name, I always will
         Love and adore!'

12   Living by Love – it's like the Magdalene
      Bathing with tears and precious perfumes there
      Your feet divine, with joyous kiss, and seen
      Wiping them gently with her flowing hair . . . .
      Then, rising up, she breaks the vase. In turn
      Your gentle Face she now embalms from this.
      My perfume, for embalming, then discern –
            My Love it is!

13   'Living by Love – what folly, how bizarre!'
      So says the world. 'Stop singing,' it will say;
      'Don't waste your life, your perfumes as they are –
      Learn how to use them in the proper way.'
      Loving You, Jesus – *loss*? But fruitful so!
      My perfumes are for You alone, that's why –
      All. And I'll sing, as from this world I go:
            'Of Love I die.'

14   Dying of Love . . . so sweet a martyrdom –
      To that I hope my suff'rings will extend:
      Cherubim, tune your lyre for what's to come –
      For this I sense: my exile soon will end.
      Love's Fire! consume me ruthlessly; I seem,
      Living at all, so burdened as I cry:
      'Jesus, my God! oh, realize my dream –
            Of Love to die!'

15   Dying of Love! Behold my hope, when hence
      I go, and see my bonds are broken: when
      My God will be my Mighty Recompense –
      I'm looking for no other Fortune then.
      To see Him, to be one with Him! May He
      Consume me (like a fire would do) above,
      Always. Behold my Heav'n, my destiny:
            Living by Love!!!

Notes

PN 17

26 February 1895

In the French, Thérèse's poetical masterpiece. It has been described as 'a "catechesis" of love', 'rich, profound and large'.

'. . . I wrote from memory, during my evening silence, the fifteen stanzas I had composed . . . during the day . . .' (*Last Conversations*, 5 August 1897).

'. . . a bit of verse for which I would willingly barter all the poetry of France': the Abbé Combes, of 'O Trinity! you are the prisoner of my love!' in stanza 2 (address delivered in the Lisieux Carmel, 30 September 1947).

St. 2, l. 2 'the Holy Name': Thérèse in fact wrote 'Parole de mon Dieu'.

St. 3, l. 1 Thérèse, in writing 'vivre de ta vie', alludes to the thought expressed by St Paul: 'And I live, now not I, but Christ liveth in me' (Gal. 2:20).

l. 2 Lit., 'Glorious King, delight of the elect.'

St. 4, l. 3 'another hill'. Thérèse says specifically 'Calvary'.

l. 5 'shout aloud and sing': joy, exuberance. Lit., 'live a life of enjoyment' (*vivre de jouissance*).

St. 12, l. 5 '. . . what does it matter that our vases be broken . . .?' (Thérèse, letter to Céline, 19 August 1894.)

27. WHAT I LOVED . . .

The Canticle of Céline

1   Oh, how I love the memory
Of blessèd days in infancy –
My innocence a flower He guarded . . . He
Surrounded me, the Lord above
With love!

2   Yes, I was little: nonetheless
My heart was filled with tenderness –
This love it had, it could not but express:
My promise to the King of Heav'n
Was giv'n.

3   Through springtime, still, how dear to me
Would Mary and St Joseph be!
So deep-immersed I was, as in a sea,
My eyes caught Heaven's blue – no slight
Delight!

4   I loved the plain: in sunlit hours
I loved that far-off hill of ours . . .
The wheat! So breathless was I for the flowers! –
When these we'd gather up and bring,
I'd sing.

5   I loved to pick . . . all that was small! . . .
The grass; the cornflowers, I recall.
The violet's scent I found – and, best of all,
That of the cowslip at our feet –
So sweet.

6   The daisies, too, whose pools of white
               Made Sunday walks a great delight:
      And birds on branches, singing! And the height –
           The firmament that shone on you –
               Was blue.

7   And Christmas Eve – the night one lays
               One's shoe beside the fire-place;
      I know I couldn't wait to wake, and race
           To sing the song I loved so well –
               'Noël'!

8   I loved Mama – her smile. Serene,
               It spoke of things that were not seen:
      'My joy is in Eternity. I mean
           To go and see the God of Love
               Above.

9   'And there my angels will receive
               Me . . . with the Virgin, I believe!
      To Jesus I will offer those I leave –
           Their heaviness, when weeping starts;
               Their hearts . . .'

10   And this I loved: the Host of white
               Came in the morning, to unite
      My soul and His, paid court! And, with delight,
           I opened – flung its doors apart! –
               My heart.

11   Later, I loved what seemed to me
               In creatures such a purity.
      The *God* of Nature everywhere I'd see:
           The peace I found will never cease –
               His Peace!

12   My father, in the belvedere,
Caressed his child: how very dear
The light that flooded me! I'd go up near
And gaze at him. His hair was so
Like snow ...

13   Thérèse and I, upon his knees,
When evening came, would take our ease:
My cradle-days, you'd think, would never cease.
And still his singing-voice, so clear
I hear.

14   Reposeful memory! that brings
The vivid sight of many things:
Our suppers ... how the scent of roses clings! ...
The cheerful shrubs, in summer light
So bright.

15   In quiet, as the light grew less
I would be merging with Thérèse! –
My soul and hers would, almost, coalesce ...
It was as though one heart would do
For two.

16   And then our hands entwined, and we
Sang, both, one Sacred Melody:
A bride in Heav'n we each of us would be!
This, even then, did Carmel seem –
Our dream.

17   Then: Italy and Switzerland –
Skies blue ... ripe fruit on every hand.
But, best, to see the Holy Father stand
And look – the Pontiff-Monarch: he
At me.

18   Love made me kiss it, when I found
         The Colosseum's holy ground!
    I heard how catacomb and vault resound.
         All answered, as I went along,
             My song …

19   Joys had to end, and tears to flow,
         Alarm had seized my spirit so.
    I donned my Spouse's arms for battle, though! –
         My good, His Cross … that only brought
             Support.

20   How long my exile was: bereaved
         Of family, I grieved and grieved!
    A doe that had been wounded, I achieved
         No shelter but one wild-rose bower
             In flower.

21   One day, my waiting soul was lit
         By Mary's smile: along with it
    A spot of Mary's blood – what benefit! –
         Became a drop of milk, to feed
             My need.

22   I loved – when from the world I'd flee –
         To hear my echo, far from me.
    Tears came; I picked the flowers, could hardly see
         (The vale secluded, blossom-strown) . . .
             Alone.

23   I loved to hear the far-off bell
         (Its chime unclear) the Hours tell.
    I'd sit down in the fields when evening fell
         And hear the breezes, going by …
             They'd sigh.

24 I loved to watch the swallows dart;
    The turtledoves, that coo, apart;
  And insect wings ... I heard them stop and start –
    Loved, as a murmured undertone
      Their drone.

25 I loved the dew upon the lawn,
    Cicada-song, from hedges borne:
  And – making honey since the crack of dawn! –
    So marvellous, the virgin bee
      To me!

26 I loved to pick the heather, turn
    And run upon the moss! I'd learn
  To catch, as it vibrated on the fern,
    The butterfly, its wings shot-through
      With blue.

27 I loved the dusk; the worms that glowed:
    The night, where countless stars were sowed;
  The moon! as on the darkest blue it rode,
    A disc of silver: at its height
      So bright!

28 I cared, in my young tenderness,
    For Father, aged now ... ah, yes,
  He was my child, my riches – happiness!
    How tenderly I gave him this
      My kiss.

29 The gentle lap of wave on stone
    We loved; the growling thunder-groan:
  Deep silence ... then, the nightingale, alone –
    Out of the woods, and rising clear –
      We'd hear.

30   One day, the Crucifix he cast
      His gaze on, and he held it fast!
    Then looked at me . . . a pledge of love, his last:
      The portion given me alone –
        My own.

31   Then Jesus – for His hand was near –
      Took him who had been Céline's dear
    And bore him far above the hill that's here,
      To live beside Eternal Love,
        Above.

32   Now I, who fled the groves, belong
      Here – in Love's Prison (and it's strong!).
    I saw that things on earth do not last long,
      My joy in them would not abide:
        It died.

33   All crushed, the grass on which I'd stand,
      The flower has withered in my hand . . .
    I'll run – I beg! – upon Your meadow-land;
      My steps won't mark it as they fall
        At all.

34   Now – as the stag, in burning heat,
      Sighs for the water, flowing sweet,
    Jesus! I run to You, on falt'ring feet:
      I need Your tears – a desert pool,
        To cool.

35   Love draws me on, and they remain
      Behind, my flock upon the plain.
    Bestir myself to guard them? I refrain! . . .
      I only want to please the new
        Lamb, You.

36   You, Jesus, are the Lamb I love
      (And on that best one *can't* improve!);
In You, I've all: the earth, and Heav'n above.
      The Flower I pick, my King, is . . . who
          But You!

37   *You*, Lily of the Valley! By
      Your perfume I am charmed. I cry:
'Bouquet of myrrh, O wreath of petals, I
      Would love and keep You – on my heart,
          Apart.'

38   Your love is always here! In You,
      I've, still, the countryside I knew –
Woods, meadows, reeds . . . the mountain, too;
      The heav'ns . . . their rains: the flakes of snow
          That blow.

39   Yes, everything! the grain that grows;
      Half-opened flowers – I've all of those:
Forget-me-not, and buttercup, and rose,
      The lily-spray, by breezes bent –
          All scent!

40   I've Solitude, whose strings can tell
      How cadences in Quiet dwell.
I've streams, and rocks, and waterfalls – gazelle! –
      I've squirrels, bucks: and, living here,
          Roe deer;

41   Horizon; greenness; coloured bow-
      Up-in-the-sky; the pure-white snow;
      The butterflies! and harvest overflow:
Far isles; and all the joy Spring yields
          The fields.

42   Still – in Your love – I'm seeing, clear
          The palms, whose tops as gold appear,
           At night, as well as when the dawn is here;
         The brook, its gentle murmurs heard;
             The bird.

43   I've grapes I see and taste, anew;
          The dragonfly – delight to view!
        Strange-flowering virgin forest. Children, too,
          That sing; their heads hair-aureoled
             With gold.

44   In You, the springs, the hills, are mine:
          The water-lilies: still entwine
        The honeysuckle . . . hawthorn, eglantine;
          And periwinkles! Poplars high
             Still sigh . . . .

45   And wind-crazed oats, that shake and cower;
          The gale that's solemn, full of power;
       Gossamer; fire ablaze; the shrubs in flower:
          The breeze, so gentle from the west;
             The nest.

46   In You, the lake; the silent wood
          Which right across the valley stood;
       The wave that spreads on sand its silver flood;
          Fish, and the treasures, brown and gold,
             Seas hold.

47   The vessel leaving harbour for
          Its path of golden tide; the shore;
       Festoons of red the clouds above us wore
          The hour the downward sun retires:
             Its fires.

48   The dove, of softest purity . . . .
          Under my habit, giv'n to me,
In You, I've necklace, ring, and finery.
      Gems – pearls and diamonds – all are mine:
          They shine!

49   The shining star: Love doesn't fail
          To give its tokens often – they'll
Disclose themselves! I see, as through a veil,
      When dusk is spreading on our land,
          Your hand.

50   You all the worlds there *are* sustain,
          Deep forests for the earth ordain
(You blink Your eye, and they give shoot again!) –
      It's following my every move,
          Your Love!

51   And I've your Heart, your Face – You show
          That gentle gaze that wounds me so;
And, Lord, Your sacred lips that kiss me. Oh,
      Jesus, I love You. I'll pursue
          But You.

52   I'll sing the praise of sacred love
          Beside the angels, up above.
And soon, I beg you, Jesus, may it prove –
      Oh, let me die of love one day,
          I pray.

53   Flame-drawn, the little moth (oh, see!)
          Becomes a flame itself. To be
The same, my soul – Your Love is drawing me –
      Would fly to You, and in its turn
          Would burn!

54   I hear, O God . . . yes, even now –
       Your Heav'nly Feast is ready! How
       (My harp hung mute upon the willow-bough)
       I'll rush – Your knees I'll scramble to! –
       To You.

55   And I'll see Mary, near You; there
       My family . . . the Saints. That's where
       I'll find again – my exile over, share
       That Home within the Father's Love
       Above!

Notes

PN 18

28 April 1895

'It now remains for me to speak of my dear Céline, the little companion of my childhood . . .' (*Aut.*, Ms. A).

Though this poem draws on Céline's thoughts and is written as though the 'I' were Céline, it echoes with memories of Thérèse's own life: her early childhood, the Sunday walks in Alençon 'when Mama used to accompany us'; Les Buissonnets in Lisieux, where 'my life was truly happy'; the 'shoe beside the fireplace' on Christmas Eve (occasion of the significant 'grace of conversion' after Midnight Mass) – though *this* shoe is Céline's, at Alençon; the trip to Switzerland and Italy in 1887: and Céline and she – confidantes of each other's thoughts – seeing in the belvedere the 'white moon rising gently over the tall trees'.

Two years after this, Thérèse sent ten of the stanzas (with slight variations of wording) to the Abbé Bellière, under the title *Whoever has Jesus, has all.*

St. 3, l. 4 'caught Heaven's blue', i.e. reflected the blue of the Heavens.

St. 5, l. 1 'all that was small': Thérèse uses the diminutives 'herbettes' and 'fleurettes' for grass and flowers, going on to specify 'cornflowers'.

St. 9, l. 1 'my angels': the four children who had died in infancy.

St. 10, l. 2 'in the morning': French 'the morning of my life'. The stanza refers to First Communion.

'to unite': see Thérèse's description of her own First Communion in *Aut.* (Ms. A).

St. 14, l. 4 'shrubs': in the French, *Les Buissonnets*, 'the little bushes'; the name of their family home, which this line says was 'full of gaiety'.

Sts. 17–18 The pilgrimage Louis made, with Céline and Thérèse, in 1887.

St. 19, l. 2 'alarm': a reference to the illness of their father, Louis Martin.

St. 21 This stanza alludes to a dream Céline had, on the Feast of the Motherhood of Mary, 1893, in which 'the Blessed Virgin came to me . . . a drop of blood pearled one of her fingers . . . I put the drop to my lips, but at once . . . it changed into milk.'

St. 32 begins the part of the poem referring to Céline after her entry into Carmel.

St. 36, l. 2 Lit., 'You are enough for me, O supreme Good!'

ll. 4–5 Thérèse quotes words written by Céline herself in an unsuccessful attempt at a poem.

St. 44, l. 1 'springs', i.e. of water.

St. 50, ll. 4–5 The French speaks of God's constant 'gaze of love'.

28. THE ATOM OF JESUS-THE-HOST

*Thoughts of Sister St Vincent de Paul, put
into words at her request.*

1   A speck of dust (not more), I've made
     My place – from which I do not stir –
     The sanctuary's holy shade,
     So close there to Love's Prisoner.
     From other loves my soul is free –
     It's set on Him whom I love most:
     The Hidden God attracting me,
     I am an atom of the Host.

2   Not knowing or forgetting there
     Created things, I silent come
     As comforter of Jesus where
     He waits in the ciborium.
     For, saving souls – that sinners live
     And come to You – is my desire:
     I beg You, to Your 'atom' give,
     Sweet Host, an apostolic fire.

3   If all the world looks down on me,
     If I'm regarded as a nought,
     God's Peace yet floods me, like a sea –
     I've Jesus there as my support.
     He never turns me from His door.
     My glory, and my innermost
     Desire is to be nothing, for
     I am an atom of the Host

4   If sometimes when the skies are made
Pitch-dark, the atom cannot soar,
She loves to hide within the shade —
Stay fixed beside the golden door.
Then will the Heav'nly Light transform
(The Blest by it are God-engrossed):
It comes upon the earth, to warm
The feeble atom of the Host.

5   Beneath that warmth of grace, its ray,
The atom sparkles and we see
When little breezes blow its way
It sways with them, composedly.
Of what, in that most sweet of states
Can it (this speck) not humbly boast?
Right up to Jesus infiltrates
The feeble atom of the Host.

6   So of my life, which round about
Love's tabernacle burns, I say:
'It wastes away, it's flowing out
As one awaits the final day.'
When trial's over, there's the tryst —
She'll soar to the Abode Divine;
The atom of the Eucharist
Near Jesus, by His side, will shine!

Notes

PN 19

Perhaps Summer 1895

When Sister St Vincent – and Thérèse, putting the Sister's thoughts into words – speak of 'an atom of the Host', that is not to be taken literally. Every particle of the consecrated Host is Jesus, undivided and entire. I think the Sister's (purely devotional, but deep) idea was her own way of expressing an intense desire to be made one with the Living Presence in the tabernacle.

Also, an atom is little. 'Oh yes, Pauline, I want always to be a LITTLE grain of sand . . .' (Letter of Thérèse, 27 March 1888).

St. 1, 1. 3 'the sanctuary's holy shade'. 'Who among is does not remember our good Sister St Vincent de Paul bowed-down by the communion grille during the whole of the evening hour of silence?' (From this Sister's obituary circular).

1. 6 Lit., 'Ah! my soul longs for the Host'

St. 3, 1. 5 Lit., 'When I approach the ciborium, all my sighs are heard.'

St. 4, 1. 4 'the golden door', i.e. of the tabernacle.

29. MY HEAVEN HERE BELOW

1   Your picture, Jesus, like a star
Is guiding me! And, ah, You know
Your Features – grace itself they are –
To me, are Heaven here below.
Your weeping . . . that to Love appears
As ornament – attractiveness!
I'm smiling while *I'm* shedding tears
At seeing You in your distress.

2   To comfort You, I want to be
Unknown upon the earth. Below
Your Beauty's veiled, and yet to me
Reveals its Mystery! and, oh,
Would I, to You, were flying free!

3   Your Face . . . my only Homeland, and
The Kingdom, too, where Love has sway:
And it's my smiling meadowland,
The gentle Sun of every day:
The Lily of the Valley – ah,
Its perfume's Mystery! I'm giv'n
What consolation from afar –
A foretaste of the Peace of Heav'n.

4   Your Face – repose and tenderness –
Is truly my melodious lyre . . .
Bouquet of Myrrh, I would caress
(Such gentleness do You inspire!),
That safely to my heart I'd press . . . .

5   Your Face ... ah, only that will be
The wealth I ask as revenue:
I'll hide in it, unceasingly;
Then, Jesus, I'll resemble You.
Imprint in me those traits divine
Your Gentleness of Face imparts;
Holiness, then, will soon be mine –
To You I'll be attracting hearts.

6   So I can gather souls – it's this,
A golden harvest, I desire –
Set me aflame! And, soon, in bliss,
Grant that sweet burning of Your Fire,
Your lips in an eternal Kiss!

Notes

PN 20

12 August 1895

'*O dear Face of Jesus!* in awaiting the eternal day when we shall contemplate your infinite Glory, our only desire is to charm your *Divine Eyes* in hiding our features too, so that here below no one would be able to recognize us ... your *Veiled Gaze*, that is our *Heaven, O Jesus!*' (Conclusion of Thérèse's Act of Consecration to the Holy Face, August 1896.)

The picture mentioned is one of the Veil of Veronica, on which, according to tradition, the thorn-crowned face of Christ was imprinted at the time of the Passion. 'She (Thérèse) had a great devotion to the Holy Face of Jesus, and she spoke to me constantly of her desire to resemble him': Sister Marie of the Trinity to the diocesan tribunal.

30. SONG OF A SOUL THAT HAS FOUND HER PLACE OF REPOSE

Written to celebrate the entry into Carmel
of Thérèse's cousin, Marie Guérin, Sister Marie of the Eucharist

1   O Jesus, it's today ˈ you break my bonds, and I
Know why this Order here ˈ – the Virgin Mary's – drew
Me to this quiet place: ˈ I'll find *true good*; that's why
I've left (though they're so dear) ˈ my family, for You:
Celestial favours, though, ˈ their recompense will be.
And sinners pardoned! – *that* ˈ is what You'll give to
   me.

2   Carmel's my chosen home, for so
Oases draw! Your Love
                            now calls me! I declare:
   It's there, it's there, that I want to go,
   To love You, love and then die.
   It's there I'd follow You – oh,
   It's there, it is there!

3   O Jesus, it's today ˈ You make my waiting cease.
Now I can be before ˈ the Eucharist engrossed,
Can immolate myself, ˈ awaiting Heaven's peace;
And, open to the Sun, ˈ the heart-rays of the Host,
In loving You as though ˈ a Seraph, I will stay:
Lord, in this hearth of Love ˈ I now will burn away.

4   Soon, Jesus, I must follow, to
        Eternal shores, from earth:
                        to me may it be giv'n
        Always to live in Heaven, with You,
        To love, no longer to die . . . . :
        Always, in Heaven with You –
        In Heav'n! yes, in Heav'n! . . .

Notes

PN 21

15 August 1895, Feast of the Assumption

'It's in your footsteps . . . that I would like to see my little Marie walking. You will be her model! Poor child, how hard these last days are for her! . . . It seems to me that the time [Marie Guérin's entry into Carmel] will never come, yet it is approaching with great strides. I ask the good God that she may be a holy religious like you, Thérèse.' (Letter to Thérèse from her aunt, Céline Guérin, 28 July 1895.)

The title given to this poem on its original publication was 'You have broken my bonds, O Lord!', taken from the first line.

St. 3, l. 1 'make my waiting cease': lit., 'fulfil all my desires' (*combles tous mes vœux*).

l. 2 'engrossed', lit., 'in silence'.

31. TO MY DEAR MOTHER, THE LOVELY ANGEL OF MY CHILDHOOD

Written for the thirty-fourth birthday of
her sister, Pauline.

1   Though far from Home (that wondrous Land),
I'm not alone, for here below
An Angel, with her gentle hand,
Protects and guides me as I go.

2   This lovely Angel-Mother sat
Beside my cradle; and the way
She sang . . . so beautifully – that
Seems just as new to me today.

3   How charming Jesus is, she'd sing –
What happiness the pure are giv'n.
Drying my tears, as with a wing,
She'd sing about the blue of Heav'n.

4   Of the Almighty, who had made
The flowers, the golden stars at night,
She sang. (He comes to childhood's aid,
This God, who keeps the lilies white.)

5   Then, of the Virgin Mary, and
Of her vast mantle, azure blue:
A hill, the Lamb – in meadowland
With virgins as His retinue.

6   This Angel – oh, what mystery –
Called *me* her little sister! Those
Motherings made her heart for me
A shelter where I'd take repose.

7   I quickly grew, beneath the white
Enclosure of these wings of yours:
The child you taught had found delight
Thinking of those eternal shores.

8   I would have left – a wish of mine –
To fly up with the Angel! Thus
In Heav'n I'd see the Light Divine
Enveloping the two of us.

9   Alas, this Angel didn't bear
Her sister up to Heav'n; she spread
Her wings . . . To seek the virgins there,
To Carmel's heights she flew instead.

10   Ah, I'd have liked to follow – see
Her virtues; being at her side,
Living the life *she* led, I'd be
Made one with Jesus as His bride.

11   And now – a wholly happy state –
Jesus has granted my desire:
Near her, in Carmel, I await
Heaven – for only that is higher!

12   I hear her sing . . . my heart is light
(I hear it daily as one prays);
And then my spirit, in the height,
With love of Him is set ablaze.

13   Love, Mother, gives me wings: I sense
That soon I'll fly! when Jesus wills
To call me, in His mercy, hence –
Winging to the Eternal Hills.

14   But – eyes set on this foreign land –
        Not leaving His bright Court, I'll burn
        To come down near my Mother, and
        Become *her* angel in my turn.

15   Heav'n won't have any charms for me
        Unless – consoling you – I will
        Change then your tears to smiles, and be
        Telling you all my secrets still.

16   Without you, Heaven's joy profound
        Would be no thing to revel at!
        Your staying long on earthly ground –
        Oh, no! I couldn't suffer that.

17   We'll fly behind the azure sphere –
        Up to our Heav'nly Homeland soar.
        We two will then, my Mother dear,
        See the Good God, for evermore!!!

Notes

PN 22

7 September 1895

'O my Mother! you know that I could never tell you all my gratitude for your having guided me like an Angel from Heaven along the pathways of life; it was you who taught me to know Jesus and to love Him.' (Thérèse, letter to Pauline, 21 January 1894).

Pauline became Thérèse's 'second mother' on the death of their mother, Zélie, when Thérèse was four. As Mother Agnès de Jésus she was Thérèse's 'Mother twice over'. We who today are quick to lambast Pauline for excessive editing of Thérèse's autobiography and poems should at the same time ponder the above words of Thérèse beginning 'it was you . . .'

Pauline, wrote Sr Teresa Margaret, DC, 'guided Thérèse's spiritual life . . . (and then), recognizing that her pupil had outstripped her, quietly slipped into the background, taking the position of disciple to her former charge.'

St. 14 In May 1897, in a letter to Pauline, Thérèse reversed the message of this stanza: 'When I am far away from this sad earth, I shall be very close to my dear Mother . . . and this without leaving the Homeland, for I will not be the one to *come down*, but my little Mother will be the one to *come up* where I shall be . . .'

32. TO THE SACRED HEART OF JESUS

1   Seeking her Jesus, to the Sepulchre,
    Bent down and crying, Mary Magdalene
    Came, and the angels wished to comfort her,
    But nothing could assuage her sorrow then.
    Archangels in your splendour! it was not
    You that her loving spirit sought that day.
    To cradle there the Angels' Lord – that's what
    She'd come to do: to take Him far away . . . .

2   She came before the day had broken . . . (who
    Had been the last to leave the tomb? This one.):
    Though hidden still His light, her God *came too* –
    By Mary's love He would not be outdone!
    Disclosing first His Blessed Face, one word
    He spoke – His heart a torrent in release.
    For Jesus murmured 'Mary', and she heard
    What gave her back her happiness and peace.

3   Once, Madeleine's was also *my* desire:
    To see You and draw near You, God, I'd fling
    My heart-gaze into endless air, aspire
    To seeking there its Master and its King.
    Seeing the flowers and birds, the starry blue,
    The lucid waters, brilliant though they be,
    I'd cry: 'If I don't see my God, then you,
    Nature, are just a mighty tomb for me!

4   'My need: a heart that burns with tenderness;
    Where – ever a support – my head can lay;
    That, loving me – my frailty no less,
    The whole of me! – won't leave me, night or day.'

But no created being could I find
Who here on earth would love me deathlessly.
I must have God who put on humankind –
Became my Brother, suffering for me.

5   You heard me, only Friend I love! To be
My heart's delight, You came . . . to *die*: Your will
The shedding of Your blood – what mystery! . . .
You're living for me on the altar still.
I cannot see the glory of Your Face,
Or hear Your voice's tones – how gentle, those:
And yet, O God, I *can* live by Your grace.
Upon Your Sacred Heart is my repose.

6   Dear Heart of Jesus! tender Treasure, You
In whom, alone, my joy and hopes reside:
You charmed me in my youth (*that*, tender too!) –
Stay, up to my last evening by my side.
O Heart of Jesus, giv'n to You alone,
My life belongs to Goodness Infinite . . . .
You know – all my desires to You are known –
My wish is that I *lose myself in It.*

7   I know, in all our acts of justice, we
Have nothing that's of value to You, so
My sacrifices . . . all! as in a sea –
To give them worth – into Your Heart I throw.
You found the Angels flawed when they were tried:
In light'ning Your commandments were conveyed.
O Jesus, in Your Sacred Heart I hide:
My virtue . . . it is You. I'm not afraid.

8   I know one must – to have the power to see
Your glory – first a path of fire have trod:
My Purgatory I would like to be
Your burning Flame of Love, O Heart of God!

My exile over, I would like to make
An act of love — pure love — as I depart;
And, flying to my Homeland then, to take
A place — directly — in Your Sacred Heart.

Notes

PN 23

October or June 1895

Céline relates how Thérèse spoke to her about a kaleidoscope
they had played with when young: '. . . pretty patterns of differ-
ent colours; if one turns the instrument it produces infinite vari-
ations.' Thérèse takes the kaleidoscope to pieces and discovers
only 'some little bits of paper and cloth thrown here and there',
and three mirrors. For her this was 'the image of a great mystery.
So long as our actions, no matter how small, remain within the
focus of love, the Blessed Trinity . . . gives them an admirable
reflection and beauty . . .' (Conseils et Souvenirs).

Do good works 'continually, but do them because we love God,
not because we think they have an intrinsic value': John Beevers,
interpreting St Thérèse.

This poem, like Poem 6, was written for Sister Marie of the
Sacred Heart. On 9 June Thérèse had made her Act of Offering
to Merciful Love.

St. 3, l. 3 'endless air': lit., 'immense plain' (l'immense plaine). I
have taken this to refer to the skies, as in line 5, and Poem 58, St.
4 (la plaine azurée).

St. 4, l. 6 'deathlessly'. The French is 'sans jamais mourir': it
refers to the fact that she could find on earth, not merely no
undying love, but no person who would never die.

l. 8 Thérèse wrote of God being 'able' to suffer, having taken
human nature at the Incarnation.

St. 7, l. 5: a reference to the angels who fell when their test came.

33. JESUS, MY LOVE, RECALL!

1   Recall how from Your Father's glory You –
   From heav'nly splendours, from Your Home
     above –
   Came down to us: what did You come to do?
   To buy all sinners back, because of love.
So small, to Mary's womb
      as though to an abyss
You came, Your grandeur veiled . . .
      Infinite glory – this?
   A Second Heaven's rest
   You found: on Mary's breast –
   Ah, this recall!

2   And now recall: at Your Nativity
   The Angels, too, came down. Their praises rang:
   'To God, all Glory, Power and Honour be,
   And peace on earth to friends of God,' they sang.
For nineteen-hundred years
      You've kept Your promise, Lord:
How rich Your children! – peace
      into their souls is poured.
   I come – because Your peace,
   Prodigious, will not cease! –
   To You, my All.

3   I come; so hide me in Your swaddling-clothes –
For ever hidden in Your crib I'd stay! –
Recalling, as angelic music flows,
The gladness then of ev'ry joyous day.
The Shepherds and the Kings
          remember, Jesus, too:
In joy, they offered hearts
          in fealty to You.
      The Innocents – outpoured
      Their life-blood for You, Lord –
      All these recall.

4   Recall that Mary's arms, to You her Son
Were more appealing than Your royal throne.
And You, to stay alive, O little one,
Relied upon the Virgin's milk alone:
Oh, what a feast of love
          Your Mother gives to You,
My little Brother – may
          I, Jesus, be there too!
      Your Mother – sister – sweet
      Gave You Your own heart-beat:
      This, too, recall.

5 And Joseph, then – the humble man You would
  Call 'Father' – snatched and took, by Heav'n's
   command
  You (sleeping on Your Mother's breast . . . Your
   blood
  Sought furiously!) to a foreign land . . .
 You, Word of God, and yet –
     what Mystery! – so meek
 That You kept silence – You –
     and made an angel speak.
   That far-away exile
   Beside the River Nile
    Oh, that recall.

6 Your Mother holds You, under different skies
  (I picture them at night, as cloudless blue):
  The stars of gold attract Your baby eyes;
  The moon, of silver, is enchanting You.
 That hand, caressing hers
     gave life to humankind
 As You upheld the world
     by keeping it in mind!
   Of *me* (my soul can sing)
   You thought, my little King –
    Oh, that recall.

7   Recall this too: that out of sight, alone,
     You worked (the hands of *God* worked hard!);
         You'd show
     You sought to be forgotten and unknown –
     Rejecting human ways in doing so.
     Although to charm the world
                         one word of Yours would do,
     It pleased you more to hide
                         the Wisdom that is You . . .
                     Appearing not to know! –
                     You, Lord, Almighty! . . . oh,
                         All that recall.

8   Recall: You were a nomad – You would roam,
     A stranger on the earth, Eternal Word!
     You'd nothing; not a stone was Yours, no home:
     You – shelterless as if You were a bird.
     Live, Jesus, now in *me*;
                         come, lay Your head and rest –
     My soul is ready now
                         for You to be its Guest:
                     My Love, my Saviour, come,
                     It's Yours, this heart, the Home
                         Of You my All.

104

9   Recall those signs of special tenderness
You showered on the smallest ones. I, too,
Would like to be receiving Your caress,
Your kisses: these delights I ask of You.
To come to You, in Heav'n
          where joy is shining clear,
The virtues of a child
          I'll know to practise here;
      Your Heaven, the reward
      Of 'little children', Lord –
        This, now recall.

10   Recall the one who, at the well, believed
The Stranger coming weary from the road:
The woman of Samaria received
That love with which Your breast had overflowed.
Ah, yes, I know the One
          who asked a drink of me:
He is the Gift of God
          the fount of glory: He
      Is Water that will flow
      And give me Life! I know –
        I hear Your call . . .

11   You call: 'Poor souls, so laden, come to Me;
Your burdens will be lightened soon! And learn:
You – quenched, yourselves, for evermore – shall be
Clear founts of Life to others, in your turn.'
I'm thirsty, Jesus, for
        this Water! Like a sea,
Let torrents, O my God,
        flood in and cover me –
    Love's Ocean my abode!
    I come – without my load,
        To You, my All.

12   Recall the sorry tale: this child of light
Often forgets to serve the King Above.
Oh, pity her in this her wretched plight,
Grant pardon, Jesus, from Your Heart of Love.
Oh, give me grace and skill
        to know of ways divine:
And from the Gospel's words
        may hidden secrets shine.
    Such treasure does it hold,
    I find it purest gold:
        Oh, that recall.

13   Recall that she who bore and mothered You
Has sway upon Your Heart! Of this, a sign
Is that You once, when she had asked You to,
Changed water into most delicious wine.
I beg – transform *my* works;
        let imperfection be
Perfection by Your power
        enacted at her plea.
    That I'm her child . . . oh, may
    You often, Lord, I pray,
        That now recall.

14   Recall, as well, that often You would seek
       The hills at evening, when the sun was low.
       Recall the words of love Your Heart would speak –
       Your prayer, with all the world asleep below.
Your orisons, O God,
          I offer with delight:
My prayers, my Office – *all*
          with them I can unite.
        There, near Your Heart, I sing
        My joyous offering.
         Ah, that recall.

15   And, seeing golden wheat . . . as though You'd
        count
       The harvest-ears with which a field was decked,
       You saw the sheaves upon Your holy mount,
       You murmured then the names of the elect.
To help Your Harvest soon
         be gathered, every day
I sacrifice myself:
         to You, O God, I pray
        The harvesters will gain
        From all my joy and pain:
        I beg, recall.

16   Recall: how all the angels celebrate
       (Their singing fills the vaults of Heav'n anew –
       What joy they have!) when they can contemplate
       One sinner who lifts up his eyes to You.
And I . . . I'd like to add
         to their high jubilee:
O Jesus, I will pray
         for sinners, ceaselessly.
        I came to Carmel – why?
       To people Heaven, I
        Can say! . . . Recall.

17   Recall, my God, that that exquisite Flame
You willed to light in hearts has sought me out.
That Blaze from Heav'n! – into my soul it came:
I want to spread its burnings all about.
For, just a feeble spark –
          no more does one require
(O mystery of life!)
        to light a forest fire:
        For this my strivings are –
        To make it travel far!
        Oh, that recall.

18   Recall . . . ah, what a feast that one would be
Which welcomed back, as son, the penitent!
Recall: the soul which has simplicity
Gets – every moment – *You* as Nourishment . . .
O Jesus, your Heart-beats
        a prodigal can know
(Those floods of love for *me*
        are boundless, also, though):
        My love! my King Divine,
        Your fortune now is mine,
        Jesus, recall.

19   Recall Your scorn of earthly glory; when
You showered on us miracles, You cried:
'O you, who seek the vain esteem of men,
How can you be believers, in your pride? –
My works amaze you now,
        but soon will come the hour
When friends of mine, yet more,
        work wonders by my power.'
        My Spouse, my Jesus, You
        Were humble, meek (I, too
        Must be). Recall.

20   Recall: as though inebriate, St John,
       Apostle-Virgin, rested on Your breast.
       Pure tenderness was what he lay upon:
       He understood Your Secrets in his rest.
    That Loved Disciple can
                no jealousy arouse –
   I know Your Secrets, too,
             O Lord! I am Your spouse.
       My Saviour, I'm caressed,
       I'm lulled, upon the breast
         Of You, my All.

21   Your Agony recall . . . enduring it,
       You wept; a sweat of blood began to flow:
       That Dew of love – its worth is infinite! –
       Has made a crop of virgin flowers grow.
   An angel showing then
             this harvest, You foresaw.
  What brought to your blest Face
           the joy it had before.
       And that You saw *me* so,
       Among Your lilies – oh,
         Jesus, recall.

22   Recall that Dew – its fruitfulness! – that made,
       Here blossoming, these virgin flowers of earth
       Be able to be mothers also: they'd
       Present You many hearts they bring to birth.
   I'm virgin, Jesus: I –
            mysterious, but true –
  Do this! For I bear souls
           through being one with You.
       In saving sinners, ours
       Such joy! All virgin flowers,
         I beg, recall.

23   Recall – in sweat and blood and suffering
A Man condemned to death lifts up His eyes,
And: 'In my power, and *soon*,' declares this King,
'You'll see me, glorious in Paradise.'
This man, the Son of God! –
                 but who believed it? Men
Did not desire to, with
           His glory hidden then.
        The Prince of Peace, who dies! . . .
      I look, and recognize
        You as my All.

24   Recall: Your Face – the Face of God – would be
Unrecognized by those who were Your own.
You've left Your lovely portrait, though, for me:
I've recognized You. You are not unknown.
I recognize You – yes,
             Eternal One! Your Face,
All covered up by tears
           has won me by its grace . . .
      Your tears (as in a cup)
      Hearts, loving, gather up –
      Jesus, recall.

25   Recall that plaint – of love for us, that came
From You upon the Cross: for, out it burst,
Escaping from Your Heart. In me, the same
Imprints itself! I share that burning thirst.
The more I feel Your Flame,
           the more I've got to do
To slake the burning. How?
           In giving souls to You!
      That thirst of love, I say,
      Burns in me, night and day –
      Oh, that recall.

26   Recall, O Jesus, Word of Life, to show
      Your love, You died for me! and so I, too
      Wish in return to love *You*, madly – oh!
      I, also, wish to live and die for You.
   You know it, O my God!
                 my one desire's to make
   You loved, and then to be
                 a martyr for Your sake.
             Of love I wish to die:
             Lord, that I want this, I
                 Beg You recall.

27   Recall this, too: 'How happy, anyone' –
      You said to us, Your Victory achieved –
      'Who, though he has not yet beheld the Son
      As gloriously risen, has believed.'
   In peace – adoring You
                 in dark but loving state,
   I'll see You when it's dawn,
                 O Jesus! – I will wait.
             My wish, my Lord so dear,
             Is not to see You *here* –
                 Oh, that recall.

28   You couldn't leave us orphans, though You were
      Ascending to the Father. In disguise,
      You stayed and made Yourself our Prisoner! –
      You veiled Your Godhead's glory from our eyes.
   And yet that veil, that shades
                 is pure and luminous:
   Faith says: 'The Bread of Heav'n
                 is nourishment for us.'
             Love's mystery! – I'm fed
             Each day by Living Bread –
                 Jesus . . . my All.

29   Though, Sacrament of Love, You have Your
       foes . . .
    In spite of all the blasphemies You face . . .
    You show how much You love me — for You
       chose
    To come and make my heart Your dwelling-
       place.
Divine and holy Host!
              Yourself as Bread You give:
I live — no longer I,
          it's by Your Life I live.
       Ciborium of gold
       Most dear to You, *I* hold
       Jesus, my All!

30   I hold You, Jesus — may my heart remain
    Your sanctuary: stay here, Holy One —
    This heart that wicked men cannot profane,
    A border where the flowers turn to the Sun.
White Lily — dearest Lord,
           if You should go away,
Then all my blossoms here
          would wither in a day.
       Jesus, my Lily-Flower,
       Have, always, as Your bower
       This heart, my All!

31   My wish is to console You in Your pain
      At sinners who forget You as they do.
      My only Love, oh grant me this as gain –
      To have a thousand hearts for loving You.
    Too few! Let Beauty then
                this greater grace impart:
   Give me, to love You with,
                the Heart of God – Your Heart.
       This, my desire (for I'm
       Afire, and all the time!)
         O Lord, recall.

32   Recall: in only this Your holy will
      I find that heart's-repose by which I'm blest –
      Submissive like a child, untroubled, still;
      My Saviour, drowsing in Your arms, at rest.
   Should *You* be drowsing too,
               though storms may rage around,
  I'd stay for ever thus,
              the peace is so profound!
      But, as You sleep, prepare
      My waking up from there,
         Jesus, my All!

33   Recall: the time for which I often sigh
        Is when in clouds of glory You'll descend.
        Oh, send Your angel soon to us, to cry:
        'Awake, awake, for Time is at an end!'
        And, oh, with what a rush
                I'll hurtle then through space,
   For, very near to You
                I'll go and take my place!
        That You my Heav'n must be:
        My Home, eternally –
        Oh, that recall!

Notes

PN 24

21 October 1895

Céline tells how, feeling a need to encourage herself, she asked Thérèse to write a poem detailing (as Céline later says, self-deprecatingly) the 'immense sacrifices' she, Céline, had made for Jesus. Thérèse responded with this poem detailing (as Céline put it) the immense 'sacrifices of Jesus for me.'

St. 3, l. 5 'the Kings'. Thérèse wrote '*mages*', 'wise men'.

St. 20, l. 1 'as though inebriate'. Thérèse's words were 'in a holy intoxication' ('*en une sainte ivresse*')

St. 27, l. 5 Lit., 'In the darkness of Faith I love and adore You'.

34. MY LONGINGS BEFORE JESUS HIDDEN IN HIS PRISON OF LOVE

1   O happy key, since you exist
        For this: you open, every day,
        The prison of the Eucharist.
        The God of Love is locked away!
        But I can turn the mortice (for
        My faith can do this wondrous thing),
        Can open up the golden door,
        To hide, beside my Heav'nly King.

2   I'd like to burn away, to be
        Consumed – near God by day and night;
        A steady glow of mystery,
        A sanctuary lamp, alight.
        What happiness is mine: I've flame
        Within me! . . . Daily thus can I
        Win Jesus *souls*, and by the same
        Heart's-fire He came to light them by.

3   O Sacred Altar-stone, you fill
        Me, every dawn, with envy too,
        As the Eternal, by His Will –
        A Bethlehem – is born on You.
        Then, enter in this soul (my Own,
        My Saviour!), since for You it burns:
        Far from the coldness of a stone,
        It's *that* for which Your own Heart yearns.

4   O Altar-cloth! where angels go –
How, too, I envy you in this:
I see my Jesus . . . there, as though
In swaddling-clothes, my Treasure is.
Change my heart, Mary! so I am
An Altar-cloth that's pure and bright,
Then may my heart receive your Lamb
Who hides Himself . . . the Host of white.

5   Paten, I envy you as well! –
Upon you Jesus takes His rest:
May Endless Grandeur come and dwell
(Though poor the lodging) as my Guest . . .
Yes, here in me – He doesn't wait
Until the dusk of life I see:
He comes, and – how my joy is great! –
A living Monstrance makes of me.

6   And how I envy you your prize –
The Blood of God, O happy Cup!
But I, too, at the Sacrifice,
Those precious drops can gather up.
Much dearer Jesus values me
Than golden vessels, jewel-set:
The Altar a new Calvary,
His Blood for me is flowing yet.

7   I am (O Jesus, Holy Vine,
To whom our fruitfulness is due)
A bunch of grapes – O King Divine! –
That ought to disappear for You.
It's in the Winepress – Suffering –
That I'll be proving what I say:
The joy of love to which I cling
Is self-oblation, every day.

8   That I should have been chosen there
      Among the grains of purest Wheat,
      That I may in their dying share,
      For Jesus: thus my joy's complete.
      I am Your spouse: You'll always be
      My Love – come live in me! I say:
      O come . . . You have enraptured me –
      Transform me into You, I pray!

Notes

PN 25

Autumn? 1895

'By ever greater devotion to Jesus in the Eucharist Thérèse enters more fully into the way of spiritual childhood. That participation in the Eucharistic mystery brings her to the perfection of abandonment . . . In the measure in which the creature consents to "lose herself" in God, she is completely possessed by Him . . .' (Père Victor de la Vièrge, *op. cit*).

Thérèse wrote this poem at the request of Sister St Vincent de Paul: see Poem 28 (PN 19).

St. 1, 1. 1 In the French the envied key is 'little'.

1. 7 'golden door': 'golden' is not in the French: but Thérèse refers, of course, to the tabernacle and has used this very phrase for it in Poem 28.

St. 4, 1. 1 'Altar-cloth'. Thérèse says, more specifically, 'Corporal', the linen cloth on which the Sacred Host and chalice are placed.

117

St. 8, 1. 8 'transform me into You'. Thérèse uses lover's language; she is not making a theological statement. She does not *really* seek a loss of her own identity, but that – her will being made one with the will of God – she be transformed into the image and likeness of God.

35. THE DIVINE LITTLE BEGGAR-BOY OF CHRISTMAS:

Extracts from a play

This play – written by Thérèse in 1895 for performance by the nuns in the Lisieux Carmel at Christmas – opens with the appearance of an angel, carrying the baby Jesus in his arms in the Bethlehem stable. He invites the nuns to come forward, one by one, to offer gifts to the Child. He specifies what gifts Jesus would most like. They include the following:

A golden throne

Jesus (your Treasure and your own!) –
Hear what to Him is very dear:
He asks of you a *golden throne*;
He finds none in the stable here.
A sinner is like that, alas –
This stable! Jesus, looking, sees
Nothing to joy His heart. He has
No place where He can take His ease.
    Save – this your goal –
    The sinner . . . his soul,
Since Jesus sighs there for His due.
    Still more – behold:
    As His throne of gold?
The *pure heart* that He wants from you!

Some milk

This Holy One – Himself their food –
Before whom saints in Heaven bow,
A Child, in His necessitude,
Is asking your assistance now.
From Heaven's bliss He came . . . I plead –
He's poor, on earth, this baby dear:
Sister, a *drop of milk* to feed
Jesus, your little Brother here!
    His smiles impart
    His words to your heart:
'That's what I love – simplicity!
    Noël, Noël!
    On the earth I dwell:
You are the milk of love for me.'

Some little birds

Sister, I see you wish to know
What little Jesus wants . . . Then I'll
Disclose it straight away, and so
I'll tell you how to make Him smile:
Go catch some *little birds*, to fly
About the stable. Doing this,
They'll represent the charm, on high,
Of children whom He loves in Bliss.
    Birdsong they sing,
    And their chirruping
Will make His tiny features shine.
    For children pray:
    In Heaven, one day,
Through *these* He will your crown entwine.

120

A star

And sometimes when a cloud of grey
Darkens and covers up the sky,
Jesus is sad, at close of day
With nothing then to light Him by.
To joy Him, let them all combine,
Your virtues, like a star at night –
A *scintillating star*, to shine:
Yes, you be now that ardent light.
    To Heaven, raise
    Up eyes; let its blaze
Tear through the veil of sinners! Ah,
    This Child that's born,
    The Planet of dawn,
Has chosen *you* to be His star.

A lyre

Oh listen, Sister, listen; may
I tell you now the Child's desire:
To have your heart, and on it play
His melodies, as on a *lyre*!
Heaven is filled with harmony
From all the holy angels: still,
Like theirs, He wants your praise to be
Sung out from here on Carmel's hill.
    Your heart is where,
    O Sister . . . from *there*
He wants the melody to rise:
    Yes, night and day,
    Love-song . . . as to say
'Here burns my life as sacrifice.'
. . . . . .

A valley

As by a blaze of sun we see
Nature is all made lovely, and
Vermilion fire gilds fetchingly
The vale of flowered meadowland,
So Jesus, Heaven's Sun divine,
Gilds all that He approaches to!
The glories of His morning shine
Brighter than fires of sunrise do.
        See Him arise,
        This Sun, in the skies! –
He sheds upon your exile dim
        His warmest beam,
        With His gifts that stream:
A *smiling valley* be for Him! . . .

Some harvesters

Below – another country there! –
Despite the snow, and winter's cold,
Protected by the Child with care,
The crops are ripening, to gold.
One needs, alas, to gather in,
Harvesters who, with hearts that burn,
Love suffering! and – souls to win –
View sword and flame with unconcern.
        Noël, Noël!
        I know very well
In Carmel you will wish this, too:
        Your Saviour pleads,
        O Sister: He needs
Many apostles, born of you.

A bunch of grapes

Sister, I wish that I were giv'n
A *bunch of golden grapes*, for I
Could then refresh the King of Heav'n —
His little mouth is very dry!
How sweet a lot is yours: regard —
You are the bunch that's pointed to:
The Child will take and *press you hard* —
His little hand has chosen you.
    Too small is He,
    Sweet darling, to be
Eating the grapes themselves, and so
    What would He choose?
    Ah, to taste the juice
From this, *His* golden honey-glow.

A little host

The Holy Child does this for you:
That He may to your soul convey
His Life, as food! transforms — into
Himself — a little host, each day.
And (with a love that's greater still)
He wants to change *you also* — yes,
Into Himself! He longs to fill
Your heart — His joy, His happiness.
    Noël, Noël!
    I come here, to tell
You what will be for your delight:
    The Lamb came to
    Be small, and to you!
Be, therefore, *His pure host of white.*

A smile

Here the metre at the end of the stanzas changes.

The world has failed to recognize
His charm (your Spouse who so endears),
And now I see – His gentle eyes
Are glistening with little tears.
Yet, you can give Him comfort who
Dear Sister, holds His arms out. So,
To charm Him, this I ask from you –
Always be smiling, here below!
For, see – does not that gaze of His
Say: 'When you look at one of these
Your sisters, and you *smile* – that is
Enough to make my weeping cease!'
. . . . . .

A flower

White snows upon the pastures reign
And cutting frost is all around:
By Winter, with its dismal train,
The flowers are withered on the ground.
Yet, see this *Meadow-Flower* appear,
Delighting you (this baby-King
Here blossoming) – from Homelands clear
Where reigning is Eternal Spring.
Be, then, a *little flower*, and hide! –
A flower that in the grasses blows:
To be beside your Spouse, beside
The King of Heav'n, the Christmas Rose.

124

Some bread

To God the Father, every day,
In prayer how often this is said –
O Author of all good, you pray,
'Give us this day our daily bread.'
God, here, our little Brother made –
He suffers now from hunger, too!
So, Sister, hear His cry for aid –
He asks *a little bread* from you.
The Holy Child, be very sure,
Wants nothing but your love. I say:
'Give food to Him – a soul that's pure,
The *bread* to feed Him, every day.'

A mirror

A mirror – what a plaything, that
For any child you want to please!
You then will find him smiling, at
The other child he thinks he sees.
Your soul's a crystal . . . come, and see
This stable, where the Word has smiled:
Here, imaged in you, may there be
His charm – the charm of God-made-child.
Ah! be, then, a reflection true,
A *mirror*, where your Spouse can trace
What He so wants: to look at *you*
And see the glory of His Face.

A palace

To house the nobles of the land
Are palaces, embellished fair;
Whilst hovels, on the other hand –
The wretched find their shelter there.
So, look at this poor stable; see
(His glory He has veiled, from love)
The Beggar-child of Christmas! He
Has left His palace up above.
You poverty (I know) embrace;
Your peace of heart is there. Ah, how
He wants yourself as dwelling-place –
A fitting *palace* for Him – now.

A crown of lilies

How sinners crown that dearest head! –
The cruel thorn around Him goes.
God's graces you should prize instead,
Of which the world no longer knows.
O you of virgin soul, may He
Forget His grief because of you:
Give Him – His *royal crown* shall be –
Pure souls of sister-virgins, too.
Come, right up to His throne, and there,
To give this Child such pleasure, braid
A beauteous crown for Him to wear:
A crown of *shining lilies* made!

Notes

RP 5 (extracts)

Christmas 1895

'See then, all that Jesus asks from us, He has no need of our works, but only of our love, for the same God who declares that *He has no need to tell us if He is hungry* is not afraid to *beg* a little water from the Samaritan woman . . . it was the love of His poor creature that the creator of the Universe was asking for' (*Aut.*, Ms. B).

In performing this play or 'pious recreation', the nuns of the Lisieux Carmel were allocated their individual stanzas by lot. That headed *A bunch of grapes* fell to Thérèse's lot.

Stanza headed *Some milk*, *ll.* 1–2 lit., 'The One who feeds the elect with his Holy and Divine Essence'.

Stanza headed *Some little birds*, *ll.* 7–8 'on high/in Bliss'. I thought this to be implied, but I may be wrong; it is not explicit in the French.

Stanza headed *A little host*, *l.* 8 'His joy, His happiness' refers to 'heart'. The French says 'treasure' also.

36. IN THE EAST

1   Up in the Eastern sky appeared a light –
      We follow its mysterious wandering.
      A blessed star; there shines out from the sight
      That born upon the earth is Heaven's King!

2   Heav'n's guard is our gain . . .
              Drawn onward, our train,
              Through snow and through rain,
              By a blazing star.

3   It halts now! prepare –
              The Child, then, is there.
              In . . . adore! In prayer,
              How merry we are.

Notes

PS2

6 January 1896 or 1895

A small poem, written for the Epiphany. Perhaps unfinished, but intense and charming.

'The greatest of all beings has become the littlest. What has worked this prodigy? Love!' (Quotation from St Bernard, written by Thérèse on a breviary picture).

37. FOR THE FIFTIETH YEAR

Written for Sister St Stanislaus, probably to
commemmorate the fiftieth anniversary of her
reception of the Carmelite habit.

1   Your virtues, for the fiftieth year,
     Have sweetened by your sojourning
     Our humble little convent here –
     The palace of our Blessed King.

          Refrain:
     We sing, we sing, that happy day
     On which our eldest Carmelite
     So loved by us! came here, to stay
     As Heaven's gift for our delight.

2   For you received us all, when we
     Came here to live, as well: and, yes,
     Your kindness to us made us see
     Your love. We knew its tenderness.

3   And soon a lovelier feast, instead
     Will make us all rejoice for you:
     When, singing, we shall crown your head
     With flowers like these, but wholly new.

Notes

PS3

Probably, 15 January 1896

'Our eldest Carmelite', Sister St Stanislaus (Rosalie Guéret) was then 71; she died in 1914. Thérèse worked with her in the sacristy, and she was infirmarian during the early stages of Thérèse's illness.

St. 3, l. 1 The impending 'lovelier feast' is that of the golden jubilee of Sister St Stanislaus's profession. For it, in August 1897, Thérèse wrote a play about the jubilarian's name-saint, St Stanislaus Kostka.

38. THE ANGEL OF THE DESERT

Extract from a play, *The Flight into Egypt*

The angel:

1   I sing the Holy Family! they are
The glory that is here attracting me:
Here, in the desert . . . yet, this glorious star
Charms more than all the lights of Heav'n I see.
Ah, who could look and understand this thing? –
Among them, yet rejected by His own!
See Jesus *moving on* – yes, wandering
Upon the earth: His beauty all unknown.

2   But if the great are scornful of Your sway –
O King of Heaven, so-mysterious Light! –
Long have You been desired by hearts today;
In You the wretched find their Hope is bright.
Abyss of Wisdom! Light that ever Is!
Your gifts (which never can description fit)
You give the small, the poor – so lavish, this.
Their names in Heaven by Your Hand are writ.

3   Since in Your image ev'ry soul is made,
The ignorant – if they are *little*, too –
Share in Your Wisdom! You, to sinners' aid
Come down and save them, calling them to You.
The day will come when lamb and lion graze
Together in one pasturage, the same:
The desert – *Your Land now!* – in other days
Will more than once re-echo with Your Name.

4   Enflamed with Your own Fires, O hidden God,
       Souls virginal will burn with love, and thus
       Will rush to where Your royal feet have trod,
       And deserts of the world be *populous* . . .
       Seraphic souls – hearts blazing – will rejoice
       The angels who, like me, in Heaven dwell:
       Their hymns to God, though sung in homely voice,
       Will cause to quail the dark abyss of Hell.

5   The jealous Satan's wish is that he could
       De-people deserts with a furious curse.
       Infinite Power he has not understood –
       Of this weak *Child* . . . new to the universe!
       He has not understood the virgins who
       Have peace of spirit in their ardency.
       He has not understood their *power*, too,
       United to their Saviour, they and He.

6   Perhaps, O God, Your spouses too, one day
       Will share in Your own exile in their turn.
       The sinners, though, who've sent them all away
       Won't quench the flames of love with which they
          burn . . .
       And sacrilegious hate, a world impure,
       Can't stain that heav'nly whiteness, or affect
       The virgins of the Lord (of that be sure):
       White vesture, and its snow will not be specked.

7   Ungrateful world, your reign is ending now:
      A little Child! ... do you not see this sight –
      He's holding in His hand the martyr's-bough,
      He gathers up the lily, brilliant white,
      To give them to His virgins, as they wait –
      Their lamps of love will shine in one array.
      Do you not see? – that high Eternal Gate
      Must, for the holy, open up one day.

8   How happy the elect when they achieve
      Exchange for their *own* love! and they are giv'n
      Such beauty of appearance, and receive
      Eternity to love Him, up in Heav'n.
      No suffering! their exile ended – for
      They have attained to their repose above:
      Their exile ended – faith and hope no more –
      Joy only then: an ecstasy of love.

Notes

RP 6 (extract)

21 January 1896, Feast of St Agnes

'... you explained to me the life of Carmel, which seemed to me very beautiful! ... I felt that Carmel was the *desert* where the Good God was wanting me also to fly, to hide myself.' (*Aut.*, Ms. A.)

St. 5, l. 6 'peace'. Thérèse's word is 'solitude'; it has overtones of repose and peace.

St. 7, ll. 5–6 Thérèse uses the adjective '*fidèles*', 'faithful', for the Virgins.

39. THE RESPONSES OF SAINT AGNES

1   My Love is Christ: He is
            my very life, and He
    Is promised to me! None
            is to these eyes as dear:
    Already, of His sweet
            celestial harmony
    The melodies I hear.

2   He has adorned my hand,
            these matchless pearls are mine:
    My neck He beautified
            with strings of costly gem;
    These sparkling diamonds, too
            that now as ear-rings shine! –
    Christ gave me all of them.

3   Adorned with precious stones
            with which He's covered me,
    I wear already – look,
            it gleams! – His wedding ring:
    My virgin's mantle ... pearls
            embroider it, to be
    One mass of glistering.

4   *I'm* promised, too! – to Him
            the Angel Host obeys:
    Him they will never cease
            to serve in awe, and that
    Is how the moon and sun,
            in silence, tell His praise ....
    His Beauty wondered at.

5   Divine His Nature, Heav'n
                    His empire, and He chose
     His Mother! (virgin she,
                    and free from stain or spot).
     His Father is true God –
                    pure Spirit: never was
          A time when He was not.

6   In loving Christ (I touch
                    Him with my finger-tips),
     That loving makes me yet
                    more pure in spirit be:
     Virginity – for He
                    has kissed me with His lips –
          Is treasure given me.

7   He has already put
                    His sign upon my face
     To make no lover dare
                    to pay me his address.
     And oh! I feel a strength
                    from Him, He gives me grace,
          This King of kindliness.

8   His Blood has given me
                    such colour! and it is
     As if in the delights
                    of Heaven *now* I share –
     Already! This I can
                    take from His sacred kiss:
          There's milk and honey there.

9   And nothing do I fear –

               not sword or flame! I'm free
From all that could impair

              my peace. I do not doubt
That this great fire of love

            that's now consuming me
    Will never be put out! . . .

Notes

PN 26

21 January 1896

'My Lord Jesus Christ hath betrothed me with his ring, and like a bride hath adorned me with a crown' (Antiphon, Office of St Agnes).

'To expect that God will "fill the hungry with good things" to the point of making them self-reliant and independent of Him would be a contradiction in terms. Always God's method of enriching us is to make us more dependent, more willing to find our completion in Him alone.' (Sr Teresa Margaret, DC)

Thérèse wrote this poem for the patronal feast-day of Pauline, Mère Agnès de Jésus.

40. FEBRUARY 24, 1896

A memento of the day of Céline's Profession

1 What could I ever compare
To this lovely day of days? –
Its sweetness utterly rare,
I shall cherish it, *always*.

2 I am bound to Jesus by
That binding which Love is owed,
Because Grandeur from on high
Has made me His own abode.

First refrain
My heart, intoxicated, turns
Into one love-pulsing thing! –
For now, in this body, burns
The Heart of my Spouse and King.

3 Now exile can bring no pain,
With Him – no wish to be free,
So soft are the bonds that chain
Ah, this *Jealous God* and me:

4 O You, Jealousy Divine –
A wound! through my heart it goes.
For all my life You'll be mine,
My joy and my sweet repose.

Second refrain
Jesus, consume this self, that so
You'll be, oh, my everything!
Henceforth I would be as though
The veil to enclose my King.

137

Notes

PN 27

24 February 1896

'Memento of the most beautiful of days ... the day containing and confirming all the graces Jesus and Mary showered upon their beloved Céline ...' (Thérèse's inscription on holy picture).

The title given on the original publication of this poem was 'Sweet Remembrance'.

Second refrain, l. 2 Lit., 'Jesus alone must live in me.'

l.4: 'enclose', though allusive of the ceremony taking place, is not Thérèse's own word. However, in writing simply 'I wish to be but the veil of my King', she herself was making a play on words. Her thoughts turned from the nun's veil (on this Profession-day) to the veil of the tabernacle containing the Blessed Sacrament.

41. THE ETERNAL HYMN, SUNG FROM EXILE

1   Your bride, who's exiled here
                     upon this foreign shore,
    Can yet sing hymns of love,
                     eternal her desire,
    For, O my Jesus! as
                     in Heav'n for evermore,
    So here on earth Your Love
                     enflames her with its Fire.

2   No greater Beauty can there be
    Than You – who give Yourself to me:
          But, in return,
          My Jesus . . . see! –
    My *life* one act of love, with which I burn.

3   You (heedless of its poverty,
          To live there!) to my heart repair:
          My feeble love – what mystery! –
          Suffices, Lord, to chain You there.

4   O Love – I'm ablaze –
          This soul be Your place! –
          Come here, of Your grace.
                  Come here, *consume me*.

5   Your ardour's design
          Finds answer (it's mine):
          'The Furnace Divine
                  My deeps ever be!'

6   Now, Lord, suffering
Is pleasure! I sing;
My soul taking wing
     Towards You, I soar.

7   My Homeland alight
My joy, in the height –
As I, in delight
     Taste You evermore!

8   My Homeland alight
My joy, in the height,
     You – Love – I live for!

Notes

PN 28

1 March 1896

Thérèse said that the Director of her soul, 'who is Jesus, does not teach me to count my acts; He educates me to do *everything* for love, to refuse Him nothing, to be pleased when He gives me an opportunity to prove to Him that I love Him . . .' (Thérèse, letter to Céline, 6 July 1893).

This poem was written for the feast-day of Sœur Marie de Saint-Joseph on 19 March.

On 21 March, Mère Marie de Gonzague would be re-elected Prioress. On the night of 2–3 April Thérèse's grave illness would declare itself in her first coughing of blood.

St. 5, ll. 3–4 Lit., 'I wish to lose myself in You for ever, Divine Furnace'.

St. 7, l. 4 Thérèse uses *gouter*, in the sense of 'savour, enjoy'.

42. HOW SWEET FOR US!

Written for the Profession day of
Sister Marie-Agnès, later to be called
Marie of the Trinity.

1 How sweet for us, dear Sister, is
This radiant day of yours! We sing
'The best day of your life, is this –
Uniting you to Heaven's King.'

2 An exile, yet you're now arrayed
(Look how their splendours shine abroad!)
In spotless wedding-clothes. You've made
A self-oblation to the Lord.

3 To gaze upon your soul there came
The Blessed Trinity! You knew
That you'd received a mark of Flame –
Their Beauty was revealed to you.

4 *You* watched the Face of God, and so
You felt your heart's desire ascend
Above all things that come and go,
All things that soon must have an end.

5 You feared the world (the deluge grew
Yet higher, and the skies were dark).
You prayed, and Heaven found for you
A refuge then, in Carmel's ark.

6 Alas, poor fugitive! you had
To spread your little wings and leave.
The dove that left the ark was sad –
So long a time was she to grieve.

7   An olive-tree! Its foliage made
A perch of gleaming green for her:
It drew her on to find the shade —
The little Carmel of Lisieux.

8   And when you soon had crossed the space
You came and your requirement brought:
To take with us the lowest place —
To suffer and to love you sought.

9   Jesus Himself, upon the day
Of His Last Supper, gave the key:
'To die for those one loves — I say
No greater love than this can be.'

10   These words so kindled you — to bless
Your heart with fervour from above,
That life for life you gave (no less)
To Jesus, as your only Love.

11   O happy victim, who return
Your own oblation now, for His!
Now taste, and daily, as you burn,
His peace and joy because of this.

12   It longs for love, your soul — to come
Where Love, a star, will draw you to:
Now Love will be your martyrdom,
And Love will open Heav'n for you.

(To our Mother)
13   This, Mother, came about through you!
Today, what was it met our eyes?
A new white 'host' was lifted to
The Holy Lamb in sacrifice.

14   She'll shine, in that ciborium
          (A mystery! To you there will
          Out of this 'host', such glory come!)
          That your own heart knew how to fill.

Notes

PN 29

30 April 1896

'It is really thanks to her (Thérèse) that I succeeded in becoming a Carmelite.' In the face of 'a thousand difficulties that were almost insurmountable', only she 'consoled me, encouraged me and adroitly seized the opportunities to plead my cause before the sisters who were against me . . . On the day of my Profession, too . . . she declared to me that it was among the most beautiful days of her life; her joy seemed to equal mine.' (Sister Marie of the Trinity, deposition to the beatification tribunal).

43. COMMENT ON THE DIVINE

*In adapting a published French translation
of the Spanish poem* Glosa a lo divino *by
St John of the Cross, Thérèse added touches
that were distinctively her own.*

Supported without any Support,
Without Light and in the Dark,
I go, consumed by Love.

1   The world (to my great happiness)
Has had – for ever! – my farewells . . .
Raised up above myself, I've . . . yes,
God's my Support, and nothing else.
That which I value, I extol –
What being near to Him has taught
Is this: to see and feel my soul
Supported, but with no support.

2   I suffer, yes! from lack of Light
(Life here is short and fugitive),
At least, though, in this earthly night
In Love Celestial I live . . . .
Though on this path which leads above
Unnumbered perils may appear,
My will is to endure, by Love,
The Darkness of my exile here.

3   I know this as reality:
The good, the bad in me – the whole,
Love's Power draws profit from, for He
Into Himself transforms my soul.
Fire burns inside my soul; it came
My heart – for always! – to endue.
I walk in Love's enchanting flame.
It always will consume me through.

Notes

PN 30

30 April 1896

Having in mind passages from St John of the Cross no doubt, Thérèse in her autobiography wrote of iron which desires 'to be identified with the fire in such a way that it is penetrated by, and absorbed in, its burning substance and seems to be but one with it . . . I ask Jesus to draw me into the flames of His love, to unite me so closely to Him that He lives and acts in me . . .' (Ms. C).

The French translation from which Thérèse made her poem is one by the Carmelites of Paris, published in 1877. Thérèse used many phrases from that version (even whole lines) but achieved a polish and a vivacity which the earlier version lacked. That version – like the Spanish of St John of the Cross – has stanzas of nine lines; Thérèse's stanzas have eight.

St. 2, l. 4 Lit., 'I possess the Celestial life of Love'.

44. I THIRST FOR LOVE!

Written for Sister Marie of the Trinity
and of the Holy Face

1 You, Jesus – God – an exile here below,
Gave up Yourself to death for me, and I
Say 'Loved One! take my life, entire; for so,
For You, I want to suffer and to die' . . .

Refrain 1
Yes, You it was who gave the sign
Your words, Lord, '*More no one can do
Than die for those one loves*' enshrine . . .
        The sovereign Love of mine,
                Jesus, is You!

2 It's late, already it is evening-time;
Come, Lord, and be my Guide upon the way.
This hill that rises, with Your cross I climb:
O Heav'nly Pilgrim, close beside me stay.

Refrain 2
Now echoes of You in me ring:
To be like You is my desire,
So what I ask is suffering:
        Your words blaze up and bring
                In me their fire!

3 You've won Eternal Victory, adored
By angels, singing of it, joy-immersed:
To enter, though, into Your Glory, Lord,
It was appointed that You suffer first.

Refrain 3
For *my* sake, on this foreign shore
You were despised – what hurt You knew!
So I . . . *last place* I ask You for –
　　Wholly to be obscure,
　　　Jesus, for You!

4　　My Loved One, Your example is a call
　　To me, that I abase myself – despise
　　Acclaim. Enchanting You means staying small.
　　So I'll forget myself, to charm Your eyes.

Refrain 4
In solitude's my peace, and this
Is all I ask for. (To pursue
What pleases You – my study is
　　That only!) . . . and my Bliss,
　　　Jesus, is You.

5　　You, Mighty God, whom all the Heav'ns adore,
　　You live in *me* – a Prisoner, night and day:
　　I always hear Your gentle voice implore –
　　'I thirst . . . I thirst for Love' is what You say.

Refrain 5
A prisoner – Yours – I shall apply,
Say over in my turn, to You
Your tender plea, as Love's reply:
　　'O Loved One, Brother – I
　　　Am thirsting too!'

6   For Love I thirst! Lord, grant me, by Your touch,
My wishes, for more Fire to warm me by.
For Love I thirst – I suffer very much:
Ah! upward, to my God, I'd like to fly.

Refrain 6
Your Love – my martyrdom of fire,
No other, rises up, and through
Me rings: 'O Jesus, my Desire,
   I ask: make me expire
    From love of You!'

Notes

PN 31

31 May 1896

The title 'I thirst for Love!', which I have retained here, was that given to the poem by Thérèse's sister, Pauline, on first publication.

The month after the poem was written, Sister Marie of the Trinity herself composed – for the second anniversary of her own entry to the Lisieux Carmel – a short poem which spoke of the 'burning hearth of love' (*brûlant foyer d'amour*) that was Thérèse's heart. Thérèse, that poem says, spends all her life, night and day, in being consumed. Its concluding quatrain may be translated as:

   By the contact with her heart's-fire
   A blaze in my own heart is lit
   To consume me! and I aspire
   To the *saving of souls* through it.

'It is because she [Thérèse] considered suffering as the supreme proof of love, as the most adequate way of identifying ourselves with Christ the Saviour, and as the best means of accomplishing God's will to save souls, that she so much desired to suffer.' (Père François Jamart, OCD, citing Mgr. Combes.)

45. THAT'S HEAVEN THERE, TO ME!

1 To bear with exile, in
     this vale of tears, I need
  To have Him gaze at me,
     the Saviour Whom I love:
  That gaze (it's *full* of love)
     so charms, that I can read
  Presentiments inside
     of happiness above.
  I sigh for Jesus: He
     then smiles . . . and at the sight
  No longer do I feel
     Faith's trial, for I see
  The Loving Gaze of God,
     His Smile that's my delight –
  That's Heaven there, to me!

2 My Heaven's to draw down
     (a power for that is mine)
  To souls, to Mother Church
     and all my Sisters here,
  The graces Jesus gives
     and, ah, His Fire Divine –
  Hearts lighted in that flame
     rejoice that they are dear.
  All, all, I can obtain
     from God, Who is my King –
  In talking heart-to-heart
     within His Mystery;
  How sweet, beside the Host
     the orisons I bring:
  That's Heaven there, to me!

3   My Heav'n! To draw forth Life,
                here to the Host I come;
For Jesus, there – my Spouse –
                has veiled Himself. I dare
To come to where (so small!)
                my God has made His home –
He hears me, night and day,
                my Gentle Saviour there.
Oh, happy moment when . . .
                in tenderness He waits! . . .
He comes to me, that I
                transformed to Him can be:
This union of love
                that so intoxicates –
    That's Heaven there, to me!

4   My Heav'n . . . to sense in me
                that likeness which will say
The Mighty Wind of God
                created me. In this
My Heaven, *always* in
                His presence I shall stay,
A child – in calling Him
                the 'Father' that He is.
I do not fear the storm,
                I'm safe in His embrace;
Abandon's my sole law –
                I trust, and totally.
To drowse upon His Heart –
                the nearness of His Face –
    That's Heaven there, to me!

5   My Heav'n . . . the Three-in-One,
               the Trinity, whose seat
      Is here within my heart –
               Love's Pris'ner! Lovingly
      I'll serve You, Captive God,
               and fearlessly repeat:
      'It's given You outright,
               the love You have from me.'
      My Heaven is to smile
               at God, Whom I adore,
      And – when, to test my faith,
               a Hidden God is He –
      To suffer, *wait* until
               He'll gaze at me once more . . .
      That's Heaven there, to me!

Notes

PN 32

7 June 1896, Feast of Corpus Christi

Written for Sister St Vincent de Paul, putting the latter's thoughts into verse.

'. . . when, to test my faith, a Hidden God is He . . .' Thérèse, throughout her writings, uses the metaphors of God 'hiding himself' or 'sleeping' to denote those times (and they were not exceptional) when she had no *emotional* perception of being loved, no feelings of consolation.

To her Spouse, the Son of God Incarnate, she wishes to be the most delicately attentive of spouses. She is humorous, too. She will smile at Him, she says, instead of complaining, and even when He gives the appearance of forgetting her, she will regard that as a compliment: 'He shows me that I am not a stranger by treating me like this.' She is playful, with a spouse's naturalness: 'He will tire more quickly of keeping me waiting than I will of waiting for Him!' (letters to Pauline, January 1889 and May 1890).

St. 2, l. 7 'beside the Host'. Lit., 'very near to the Sanctuary'.

46. WHAT I SHALL SOON SEE FOR THE FIRST TIME

1   Though I am still upon this foreign shore,
I feel the stirrings of a happy state:
Oh, would I were in Heav'n, and that I saw
The marvels that are there to contemplate.
I dream of joys hereafter – that is when
My exile seems no burden! I'm serene
For soon I'll near my only Home, I then
Will fly to where, before, *I've never been.*

2   O Jesus, give me wings of white, then I
Can come to You, by soaring in the air:
To those Eternal Shores I want to fly –
I want to see You, God my Treasure, there.
I want to fly to Mary's arms – for, near
Her on her throne I'll find such rest in store.
And there she'll give to me, my Mother dear,
The gentle Kiss I've never had before! . . .

3   Loved Jesus! soon, so tenderly (above,
As never yet to me) Your smile impart,
And I, in a delirium of love
Will (let me!) hide myself inside Your Heart . . .
Oh, what a moment! and what joy to me
To hear You softly speaking. I'll adore
When first I glimpse Your Face, and in it see
That Glory which I've never seen before . . .

4   You know, O Sacred Heart of Jesus, why:
      My martyrdom's Your Love that draws me. For
      If, now, for Heav'n's delightfulness I sigh,
      It's so I'll love You, love You more and more!
      In Heav'n – as though I'm drunk with love of You
      (No laws, no limits there!) – my happiness
      As first I drink it in, will be, all through
      Eternity, so new . . . and never less!!!

Notes

PN 33

12 June 1896, Feast of the Sacred Heart of Jesus

'Ah . . . I recognize, yes! that all my hopes will be fulfilled . . . yes, the Lord will do marvels for us that will infinitely surpass our *immense desires!*' (Thérèse, letter to Pauline, 28 May 1897.)

'. . . I really find it hard to conceive how I will be able to become acclimatized in a country where joy reigns without any mixture of sadness. Jesus will have to transform my soul and give it the capacity for enjoyment, otherwise I shall not be able to bear the eternal delights.' (Thérèse's last letter to Père Roulland, 14 July 1897.)

'Never . . . been', etc.: Thérèse's precise words, repeated in each final line, are 'for the first time'.

The title given on first publication of this poem was 'My Hope'.

St. 1, l. 2 Lit., '. . . sensing eternal happiness.'

47. THROWING OF FLOWERS

1   Each evening, what a joy
           when gathered flowers are thrown,
  Spring roses . . . as I pull
           away the petal-leaf,
  My only Love! before
           your Calvary of stone,
    I'd like to wipe away Your grief . . .

Refrain 1
Throwing of Flowers – 'First ones for You!' – I
    bring
All of my lightest sighs
           and all my deepest woes:
Each little sacrifice –
           joy, pain, as offering –
    My flowers are those! . . .

2   Your beauty, Lord! – my soul's
           in love! it takes and flings
  My perfumes, and my flowers
           uncounted, to all parts:
  In throwing them for You
           upon the breeze's wings
    I'd like to be enflaming hearts!

Refrain 2
Throwing of Flowers – it arms me, Jesus! I'm
Certain that when I fight
           for saving sinners so,
I'll win. By these I can
           disarm You every time –
    These flowers I throw!!!

3   They touch your Face, the flowers;
                of this, by their caress —
'My heart is always Yours'
                these roses are a sign:
Un-petaled now . . . You know
                the thought that they express;
    You're smiling at this love of mine.

Refrain 3
Throwing of Flowers, to give you praise once
    more —
My only pleasure, that,
                through all this sad vale's hours.
I'll be in Heav'n soon, with
                the little angels, for
Throwing of Flowers! . . .

Notes

PN 34

28 June 1896

'I have no other means of proving my love for You than that of throwing flowers, that is, not allowing any little sacrifice to escape, any look, any word; to profit by every little thing and to do it for love.' (*Aut.*, Ms. B.)

Every evening during that month of June, Thérèse and the novices collected rose-petals, and, standing in the courtyard, symbolically *flung* them up high, so that some might touch the face of the metal figure of Christ on the granite cross. Can one not just see it? (Their arms go back to give impetus to each long-arced throw.)

Refrain 1, l. 1 'First ones for You!' Thérèse's phrase is 'offrir en prémices', offer as first-fruits.

48. TO OUR LADY OF VICTORIES, QUEEN OF VIRGINS, APOSTLES AND MARTYRS

Poem referring to Thérèse's spiritual support
for Père Adolphe Roulland, Priest of the Foreign
Missions, who was about to sail for China.

1   To you, my Mother – who obtain
     All that I hope for, I renew
     In love and thanks, my humble strain,
     This heart-song that is sung to you . . .

2   A missionary's work I share –
     Held fast to it by you, above:
     United by the bonds of prayer,
     And those of suffering and love.

3   *His* lot's to cross the world, it is
     Proclaiming Jesus. And, for me
     To practise humble virtues, this
     In shadows and in mystery.

4   I ask for suffering. The Cross
     I love – desire! Ah, well you know –
     To save one soul from final loss
     A thousand deaths I'd undergo!

5   A sacrifice, in Carmel, I'd
     Assist in Heaven's conquering –
     Through him, to make flare up inside
     The flames that Jesus came to bring.

6   Through him – what joy and mystery! –
        To journey to the East; I can
        Then make the tender Virgin be
        Loved, as a Mother, in Su-tchuen.

7   Mary, in my deep silence may
        I win hearts, as I want to do.
        Through your apostle, far away,
        I'll be converting sinners too!

8   Through him, baptismal water makes
        A baby of a day become
        A temple! In his love, God takes
        His place there – makes of it His Home.

9   Through him, what children's legions, I
        Am sure, will up to Heaven rise
        (Angels I want to multiply
        For populating Paradise!)

10   Through him, too, God will now bestow
        The palm for which I really sigh:
        The sister of a Martyr! Oh,
        Dear Mother, how the hope soars high!

11   The glorious battle over – and
        Our exile ended – we, elate,
        Will savour in our Native Land
        The fruits of our apostolate.

12   To him, the victor's crown, before
        The Army of the Blest arrayed.
        To me . . . *his* glory, evermore
        Reflected. It shall never fade.

Notes

PN 35

16 July 1896, Feast of Our Lady of Mount Carmel

'I ask Him that you will be, not only a *good* missionary but a *saint* all on fire with love of God and of souls; I beg you to obtain for me this love also, so that I may be able to help you in your apostolic work. You know that a Carmelite who was not an apostle would be distancing herself from the goal of her vocation and ceasing to be a daughter of the seraphic St Teresa [of Avila] whose desire was to give up a thousand lives to save one soul.' (Thérèse, letter to the Abbé Maurice Bellière, White Fathers seminarian, 21 October 1896).

Père Roulland, first, and later the Abbé Bellière, were Thérèse's 'spiritual brothers'. She corresponded by letter with both. Each had asked the Lisieux Carmel that one of the nuns support him, from afar, by her prayer and sacrifices.

For a reason that can only be surmised, Pauline reworded this poem so that it appeared to relate to *both* Père Roulland and the Abbé Bellière, but in fact it was written for the former only.

St. 4, l. 3 Lit., 'To help to save one soul.'

St. 5, l. 2 'assist in Heaven's conquering', lit., 'assist the Conqueror of souls'. Thérèse's desire is to '*spread*', through Père Roulland, the flames brought from Heaven by Jesus.

St. 11, l. 2 'elate', though archaic, *is* in the *Oxford English Dictionary*. It has the meaning of 'elated' and (almost) the sound of 'light'.

49. HEAVEN'S THE PRIZE-TO-BE

1   *Heaven's its prize-to-be!*
     Dark still, when someone brings
     The 'cudgel' round: it rings
     Its 'Get-up-quick' at me.

2   Heaven's the prize-to-be.
     Here, when we each arise,
     What marvels meet our eyes:
     Not Paris ones *we* see!

3   Heaven the prize-to-be.
     In my poor cell . . . It has
     No carpet, looking-glass;
     No tulle for drapery.

4   Heaven the prize-to-be.
     No table, not a chair:
     The lack of comfort there
     Is our felicity.

5   Heaven the prize-to-be.
     I see without alarms
     (All glitt'ring there!) my arms –
     Love their click-clackery!

6   Heaven the prize-to-be.
     All these – hair shirt; cross, chain,
     As sacrifice – are gain!
     In these my arms you see.

7   Heaven the prize-to-be.
After I've said a prayer
I kiss the floor-boards there,
Obey our Rule's decree.

8   Heaven the prize-to-be.
Armour my habit holds,
Hid in these homespun folds,
This veil that's wrapping me.

9   Heaven the prize-to-be.
If Mother Nature should
Grumble to me, I would
Answer her, merrily:

10   'Heaven's the prize-to-be!
Hungry? – too bad', I say,
'Fasting's an easy way
To more agility!'

11   Heaven the prize-to-be.
Unsparingly we feed
On carrots, cabbage, swede,
Potatoes – radish, see!

12   Heaven the prize-to-be.
At evening . . . no surprise
That – there before one's eyes –
Just bread and fruit for me!

13   Heaven the prize-to-be.
Bread passes . . . I receive
The plate of fruit but leave
The fruit, fair-mindedly.

14   Heaven the prize-to-be.
My plate – of clay not grand!
(For fork, I use my hand),
This boxwood spoon's for me.

15   Heaven the prize-to-be.
And when at last we meet
Our topic's one that's sweet –
Joys of eternity!

16   Heaven the prize-to-be.
We sew when talking, take
The scissors out, to make
New vestments carefully.

17   Heaven the prize-to-be.
And here we have the sight
Of faces all alight
With holy gaiety.

18   Heaven the prize-to-be.
An hour goes quick, and now
One, with unfurrowed brow,
Returns to hermitry.

19   Heaven the prize-to-be.
In all the cells, the cries
From penitence arise –
They really deafen me!

20   Heaven the prize-to-be.
Sixty-six thousand blows
I notch up yearly! (Those
Are quite precise, you see.)

Heaven the prize-to-be.
     We help the missions, for
     We on ourselves make war —
     Fight, unrelentingly!

Notes

PS 4

Perhaps Summer 1896

It was not without hesitation that this jokey account of daily life in the Lisieux Carmel of 1896 was here included. There is a draft in Thérèse's handwriting, but did she write the poem itself? *Un Cantique d'Amour* quotes a letter of 7 July 1896 from Marie Guérin to her mother mentioning 'my famous canticle on the life of Carmelites'. Was this it, and in what sense was it hers, Marie's?

Possibly it was a joint exercise of Thérèse and the novices at recreation? In so far as it draws attention to austerities it does not seem Theresian: but Thérèse surely wrote or had a hand in the final stanza: 'We on ourselves make war/Fight, unrelentingly!'

St. 1, l. 3 'cudgel': humorous description of what was in fact a rattle or clapper, consisting of a piece of metal on a board of wood.

St. 5, l. 3 'arms', i.e. weapons.

St. 6, l. 2 'hair shirt', etc. For the nuns such acts of physical penance were superogatory, i.e. more than duty required.

St. 20, l. 2 'Sixty-six thousand blows' per year, i.e. self-chastisement with the 'discipline'. In keeping with its whole tone, this poem treats the penitential practice semi-humorously; but the apostolic intention of aiding the spiritual combat, and especially of helping missionaries (stanza 21), by physical and other mortifications is treated very seriously.

50. FOR ST MARTHA'S DAY

*This day was traditionally celebrated by festivities
in honour of the 'sisters of the white veil', the non-choir
sisters who carried out 'Martha-like' duties in the
convent. This poem accompanied gifts to them.*

Refrain:
Most noble Sisters veiled in white,
To fête you gives us great delight.

1   Márie of the Incarnation,
    You we offer . . . navigation:
    This pretty little boat, you bet,
    Will charm the heart of Henriette.

2   Sister St Vincent, now! We choose
    A snapping dog . . . it's very spruce.
    This animal, by barking hard,
    Will be a splendid garden's guard!

3   For dearest Martha? Not so big –
    A most delightful *little pig:*
    A hunting-pig, to ride! (for that's
    The very thing for chasing rats).

4   'Baptiste' – and this will set the tone –
    Presents to Mélanie alone
    A little cat, which cannot wait
    To come up close and lick the plate.

5   A jug! . . . what *can* we say? (that touch
    Betokens we don't know too much) . . . .
    Let's scoot now – look, that's Teacher there;
    Hasn't he on his grandest air!

Notes

PS 5

29 July 1896, Feast of St Martha

St. 1 Sister Marie of the Incarnation, initial recipient of the 'pretty little boat', no doubt had a small relative, Henriette, to whom the boat would then go.

St. 4, l. 1: 'Baptiste' was Marie Guérin (Sister Marie of the Eucharist). The allusion is to the part she took in a feast-day play, that of a gardener in smock and wig. 'The Teacher', in the same play (stanza 5) was Sister Marie of the Trinity.

l. 2 Mélanie Lebon was Sister Marie-Madeleine's name before her entry to Carmel.

51. JESUS, HIM ONLY

1   My heart – it needs to prove its tenderness –
    Wants to be given *always*, and no less!
    To comprehend my love . . . who can keep track?
    What heart is there who'll want to pay me back?
    Pay back? – my claims aren't met! By none beside
    You, Jesus, is my soul's need satisfied.
    Nothing could ever charm me here below,
    True joy of heart is not encountered so.

        My only peace and heart's reward,
        My only Love, is You, O Lord!

2   Heart-fount of mother's hearts, Creative Mind!
    In You most tender Fatherhood I find.
    My Jesus! Word! Your Heart for me in this
    Is more maternal than a mother's is.
    Always You're here! You guard, You'll never be
    Late when I call and ask You 'Come to me';
    And if sometimes You seem to hide away,
    You come to help me seek You, so to say.

3   Jesus, to only You would I be tied –
    It's *Your* arms that I'm rushing to, to hide.
    For, like a child's I want my love to be –
    And like a warrior, battling valiantly:
    Yes – like a dainty child's impulsiveness –
    I'll be so lavish, Lord, with my caress,
    And in the field of my apostolate,
    A warrior, throw myself into the fight!

4   You guard one's innocence and make it whole –
     Your Heart could not deceive me! In my soul
     Is hope in You, that – exile finished – I
     Am going to behold You up on high.
     When storms of heart upsurge, I raise my head,
     Jesus, to You: and it's as though You said
     (Your gaze of mercy comes into my view,
     Saying): 'My child, I made the Heav'ns, for *you*.'

5   I know this very well – my tears and sighs
     Are radiant with charm before Your eyes.
     You have, as royal court in Heav'n above,
     The Seraphim – and yet, You beg *my* love . . .
     You want my heart – it's here! I utterly
·   Cede my desires to You. Those loved by me
     (Jesus, my Spouse and King!) are persons who
     Will only now be loved by me *for You*.

Notes

PN 36

15 August 1896, Feast of the Assumption

'Grape-shot, cannon's roar – what does all that matter when one is carried by the General?' (Thérèse, letter to Sœur Marie de Saint-Joseph, c. October 1896.)

'If the soul wants to live in *abandon*, it must not remain at the "level" of the difficulties it meets . . . Instead of battling with temptation or wanting to triumph by itself, the soul immediately rises toward its Father and relies upon Him; better still, it offers the difficulty to Him.' (Père Victor de la Vièrge, *op. cit.*): 'It's *Your* arms that I'm rushing to, to hide.'

This poem was written for Sister Marie of the Eucharist, containing thoughts of Marie's and directed towards what had been her excessive entanglement of heart with her family, the Guérins.

St. 2, l. 5 'here ... guard'. In the French, Thérèse says that at every moment Jesus is *following* and guarding her.

St. 3, l. 5 'dainty child's impulsiveness', lit., 'a child full of little attentions'.

St. 4, l. 1 'make it whole', lit., 'restore'.

St. 5, l. 5 'it's here!', lit., 'I give it to You'.

52. FEAST-DAY QUATRAINS

Written for Thérèse's cousin, the former
Jeanne Guérin, and her husband,
Dr Francis La Néele.

1   These wretched feast-day quatrains, read –
    A posy not so popular!
    For somewhere deep inside my head,
    That's where those *Alexandrines* are.

2   '*Some Alexandrines*', it was these –
    '*For Francis*' – I was told! Suffice
    To say I should have held my peace
    Before an order so precise . . .

3   My fault you won't be hard upon,
    Dear Jeanne, my Learned Sir. At least,
    Though *Alexandrine*-less, it's – On!
    To celebrate my Sister's feast.

Notes

PN 37

21 August 1896

A trifle, in response to a request by Jeanne. The feast-day is that of St Jeanne-Françoise Frémiot de Chantal, co-founder of the Order of the Visitation; Thérèse's sister, Léonie, was a nun in the Visitation Convent at Caen.

Thérèse would have presented this and the next two poems together.

171

53. JESUS'S CONFIDENCE TO THÉRÈSE

Jeanne was longing for a child.

1   O Jesus, now, for all I'm worth
    I beg, as ardent longing can:
    Exile an angel to the earth,
    And give a little child to Jeanne.

2   How long the time as we await
    That little exile out of Heav'n!
    It's strange – yet, Lord, You indicate
    To me why no reply's been giv'n.

3   Your very silence tells me why:
    'It mounts to Heaven, such distress –
    I must restrain Myself, that I
    Do not reply at once with "Yes".

4   'No ordinary angel she
    Will be receiving. I'll impart
    This, out of love, in mystery –
    The forming of her soul and heart.

5   'Myself, I now her soul attire
    With gifts, with treasures Heaven-sent.
    But in return ... ah, I require
    From Jeanne complete Abandonment.

6   'My tender hand, dispositive,
    Prepares her. So I will acquaint
    You now of this, Thérèse: she'll give
    My Holy Church a Pope, a Saint!'

Notes

PN 38

21 August 1896

A poem which is not to be taken seriously, except in its central message that God always has a good reason if He does not grant our desires in this life, though we cannot always see what that reason is.

Thérèse's whimsical 'prophecy' appears to have been based on a dream she had in 1892: in fact Jeanne and Francis never had a child. On receiving this poem Jeanne wrote to Thérèse: 'I shall ... profit from the confidences Jesus has given you, and I shall abandon myself completely to His holy will. He knows much better than I do what is necessary for me ...'

After Thérèse's death Jeanne wrote: 'The favours she (Thérèse) is granting me are much more precious than if she were to send me the little fair-haired child she promised. She consoles me spiritually, she suggests that I offer up my little sufferings for a priest ...' Subsequent to the death of Francis in 1916, Jeanne adopted one of his grand-nieces.

54. A DOCTOR, HOLY AND FAMOUS

An acrostic, the initials spelling 'Francis'.

Francis's motto, writ immense:
'Render to God, not man'; desire
All for the Church and her defence! –
Now had he not a heart on fire?
Combatting thus the impious scene,
In Faith, he raised her Banner higher . . .
Such glory! – that of Heaven's Queen.

Notes

PN 39

21 August 1896

'Francis': St Francis of Assisi, of course, but also Francis La Néele (whose Christian name was 'Francis', not 'François'; so it is 'Francis' that is spelt out in French too). Thérèse's sister Pauline had included the motto 'Nothing to men, all things to God' in a decorated greeting given to Jeanne and Francis on their marriage.

In September of this year, 1896, Thérèse will write 'Manuscript B': 'I will be love within the heart of the Church . . .'

Line 5 'impious scene', lit., 'impious science'. Francis, Dr La Néele, a combatant against secularist prejudice, had recorded the miraculous cure of one of his patients at Lourdes.

Line 6 Lit., 'He made avowal very loudly.'

55. THE SACRISTANS OF CARMEL

1   No job we do could be as nice.
     We tend the altar, and prepare
     The bread and wine: the Sacrifice
     Will give to earth . . . ah, 'Heaven' there!

2   Yes, Heav'n – oh, highest Mystery –
     Which under *bread* has hid away.
     For Heav'n is simply Jesus: He
     Comes to us here, and every day.

3   Could ever queenly joy compare
     With that which *our* pursuit allows?
     This job we do – it is a prayer,
     One that unites us to our Spouse.

4   Should honours of the world abound
     They'd be as nothing, now, to us
     Who've peace – celestial, profound –
     Which Jesus makes us savour thus.

5   We bring a holy appetite
     To what our works-of-hand entail,
     To make the little hosts of white –
     The Lamb of God they're soon to veil.

6   This, Jesus, Spouse and Friend, inspires
     (Who chose us in His love) to tell:
     That we are hosts and He desires
     To change *us* into Him as well.

7   O Priestly mission, high and grand,
You become ours on earth today! –
The Master has transformed us, and
He guides our steps upon the way.

8   As prayer, as love, is made to count
In what apostles shall have wrought,
Their fields of combat ours, we mount
Our daily fight in their support.

9   This God, whom tabernacle hides –
Our hearts, as well, He's hiding in.
We pleading – wonder! He provides
For sinners a release from sin.

10   Our happiness and glory's sum –
To work for Jesus and His goals.
His Heav'n is a ciborium:
We wish to fill it up with souls!

Notes

PN 40

November 1896

In Manuscript B, Thérèse wrote: 'Without doubt, these three privileges are indeed *my vocation, Carmelite, Spouse and Mother*' [of souls]. She then lists other things she felt drawn to ('I feel in me other *vocations*'): WARRIOR, PRIEST, APOSTLE, DOCTOR, MARTYR; 'I feel in me the courage of a Crusader, of a Papal Zouave . . .'

If she were a priest, she muses, 'with what love, O Jesus, I would carry You in my hands when, at my voice, You would come down from Heaven ... With what love I would give You to souls!' That said, in the next breath she *puts aside such feelings, giving humility as her reason for doing so:* 'But alas! all the time I want to be a *Priest*, I admire and envy the humility of St Francis of Assisi and I feel in me the *vocation* of imitating him in refusing the sublime dignity of *the Priesthood.*' Thérèse cannot be cited in support of the controversialists, the feminist pressure groups.

Four years before, she had written: '... our mission as Carmelites is to form those labourers in the Gospel who will save thousands of souls, whose mothers we shall be ... I find our portion very beautiful, what have we to envy in priests?' (letter to Céline, 15 August 1892).

Thérèse's words in stanza 7, lit., 'Sublime mission of the Priest, you become ours [the nun-sacristans'] here below' are a devotional analogy or metaphor. She poetically represents the sacristans as altar-breads (stanza 6) 'transformed by the Divine Master' (stanza 7).

St. 2, l. 2 'under' (*sous*) bread, i.e. under the appearance of bread.

St. 5, l. 1 'appetite': Thérèse uses the word *envie*, 'desire' or 'longing'.

l. 3 'little hosts of white'. This refers to the altar-breads, which were made in the Carmel itself.

St. 9, ll. 3–4 Lit., 'at our voice ... (He) deigns to pardon sinners.'

56. HOW I WANT TO LOVE

1 Jesus my God, I'm praying now to tell
   You of my love by which I would impart
   Such joy to You alone (You know this well –
   Oh, grant the ardent longing of my heart!).
   I'll bear the trials of this exile, for
   That is a way to charm and comfort You.
   Change into Love (O Saviour, I implore)
   Each little task that I, Your spouse here, do.

2 Yours, Jesus, is the Love that I desire!
   It's that which must transfigure me, for when
   You fill my heart with Your consuming fire . . .
   Do that, and I can bless and love You then.
   Then how I'll love You! how I'll bless Your Name
   Just in the way that those in Heaven do:
   Yes, Jesus! with such Love – the very same –
   As I received, Eternal Word, from You.

3 My God and Saviour, at my dying breath
   Come, seek me, with no shadow of delay.
   Ah! show me such great tenderness in death,
   Your gaze that's full of gentleness, and say
   With love – oh! let Your voice be calling me
   To whisper 'All is pardoned', and Your touch
   Say 'Rest, my faithful spouse, and come and be
   Caressed upon this Heart you've loved so much!'

Notes

PN 41

End of 1896

'I understood that there were many degrees of perfection and that each soul was free to respond to the advances of Our Lord, to do little or much for Him, in a word, to *choose* among the sacrifices He asks. Then, as in the days of my babyhood, I cried out: "My God, *I choose all!*" I don't want to be a *saint by halves . . .*' (Ms. A).

Poem written at the request of Sister St John of the Cross.

The title given to this poem on first publication was 'Still a Song of Love'.

57. SWEET CHILD, MY NAME
YOU KNOW

*Thérèse imagines herself in a boat
with the Holy Child.*

1   Sweet Child! . . . ah, my name you know;
    Your loving gaze at me here
    Says 'Your worries on *Me* throw,
    Just that, it is I who'll steer!'

2   With little hand uplifted, You
        Can quiet the sea –
    O marvel! . . . winds uproaring, too
    I've heard Your little voice subdue
        As they blew.

3   If you want to rest and stay
    As the thunder-rumbles scold –
    Upon me, I beg you! lay
    Your head's little locks of gold.

4   How sweet your smile in sleep! And who
        Is there who would be
    Not moved to sing what I've in view . . .
    Tenderly as one's able to,
        Rocking you.

Notes

PN 42

December 1896

'My Céline ... is ... in a small boat, *land* has disappeared from her sight ... the helm, which Céline cannot even glimpse, is not without a pilot. Jesus is there, *sleeping* as once He did in the boat of the Galilean fishermen ... The wind blows ... yet if He awoke, but for an instant, He would have only to "command the wind and the sea" ... The apostles have given Him a *pillow* ... But in His dear *bride's* little boat Our Lord finds another pillow much softer; it is Céline's *heart* ...' (Thérèse, letter to Céline, 23 July 1893).

The parallels between the letter and the poem are strong. But in the poem Jesus – strong helmsman there, as in the letter – is the Child of Bethlehem. Paradox of the Incarnation!

The title given to this poem on first publication was 'To the Child Jesus'.

St. 1, l. 3 'your worries on Me throw', lit., 'simple *abandon*'.

St. 3, l. 2 'thunder-rumbles scold': Thérèse's verb *gronder*, scold, also describes what thunder does; it rumbles or growls.

58. THE AVIARY OF THE CHILD JESUS

1   For exiles here, His love to show,
     God made the birds whose chirping fills –
     Birds *pray* so, going to and fro –
     The valleys and the sides of hills.

2   Joyfully, flighty children choose
     The ones they like, and then they hold
     Them prisoners in cages – whose
     Bars have been painted all in gold.

3   Our Little Brother thus to be,
     Jesus, You've quitted Paradise.
     Yet, Holy Child, Your aviary –
     Carmel, of course, that signifies.

4   Though *our* cage isn't golden, we
     Are fond of it, and by His grace
     We never hanker to be free
     To seek the woods, the azure space.

5   In this world's groves find our content?
     There, Jesus, we're not able to!
     Our lives in deep seclusion spent –
     Thus we would sing, and just for You.

6   Your little hand, dear Child – it takes
     Our hearts . . . ah, how your charms endear!
     And, Jesus – God – your *smile!* It makes
     The little birds your captives here.

7   The soul in its simplicity
Finds here the object of its love.
The vulture will no longer be
The terror of the timid dove.

8   One sees it – on the wings of prayer
The ardent heart is soaring high,
As when the lark – in upper air –
Sings as it rises in the sky.

9   What song – as in their cage they stay –
From wren and merry chaffinch pours!
O little Jesus, listen: they
Chirp out Your name, these birds of Yours!

10   The little bird, on singing bent –
No troubles in *his* life appear:
A grain of millet – he's content!
He never has to sow it here.

11   And to *our* aviary You bring
All that we need. What we've to do –
The only necessary thing,
O God and Child! is loving You.

12   As well, we sing Your praises: so
With those pure-spirits up above
Unite. The birds of Carmel know
The angels look at them, and love!

13   Jesus, to wipe away Your tears
(Which sinners cause) Your birds repeat
Their song – about Your charms. One hears
Them gain You hearts by singing sweet.

14   From this sad world, one happy day
              You'll call them! Through the aviary door,
              Full opened, then they'll fly away:
              All of them, up to Heaven soar.

15   In Heaven's heights, we'll fly among
              The joyous little cherubim:
              And greet the Child Divine! The song
              We'll sing then is in praise of Him.

Notes

PN 43

Christmas 1896

'From the time of my departure from the boarding school, I installed myself in *Pauline's* old painting-room and arranged it to my taste. It was a real bazaar, a collection of pious objects and curiosities, a garden and an aviary ... I had a table on which was placed a *large cage*, containing a *large* number of birds, whose melodious song deafened the ears of visitors, but not those of their little mistress who cherished them very much ...' (Thérèse at Les Buissonnets: Ms. A).

'Immensity will be our domain ... we shall no longer be prisoners in this land of exile ... *everything* will have PASSED!' (Thérèse, letter to Céline, 12 March 1889).

St. 3, l. 2 'You've quitted Paradise'. The sense (and grammatical tense) of immediacy comes from the fact that Thérèse wrote this poem for Christmas.

St. 12, ll. 3–4 Lit., 'all the angels love the birds of Carmel'.

59. TO MY LITTLE BROTHERS IN HEAVEN, THE HOLY INNOCENTS

*There is perhaps a secondary allusion to
her own two sisters and two brothers who
died in infancy.*

1   Oh happy Little Ones! –
                ah, with what tenderness
         Did Heaven's King
  Bless you! He on your brows –
             to joy you – His caress
        Was lavishing.
  (All Innocents do you,
             in figure, comprehend);
        Reflection brings
  A glimpse of what in Heav'n
             You're giving, without end,
        O King of kings.

2   Such riches you have seen
                (dear little Lilies), there
        In Paradise –
  Before you had to know
             the wretchedness *we* share,
        You've won the prize!
  O scented buds the Lord
             has gathered at the hour
        Of morning dew,
  What gentle Sun of Love
             knew how to make you flower? –
        His Heart: It knew.

3   Such *care* does Mother Church
                    (in honouring your birth,
            Your death) display!
    What loving tenderness
                    for you whose life on earth
            Was but a day . . .
    For – in her Mother's arms;
                    first fruits of Harvest – she
            Thus offered you
    To God: and what delights,
                    eternally, you'll be
            In Heaven's blue!

4   You, virginal, the Lamb
                    accompany and praise:
            O Children, we
    May hear you singing there
                    (an honour to amaze)
            New melody.
    O conquerors, you've won
                    strange glory that without
            Combat occurs.
    For you the Saviour put
                    the enemy to rout.
            Sweet vanquishers!

5   No precious stones your hair
                          illuming, does one see
                 The Heavens hold:
      Reflected – a delight
                          of silkiness! – will be
                 Your locks of gold . . . .
      The palms, the crowns that are
                          the treasures of the Blest –
                 You have all these . . .
      And, children, in your Home
                          rich thrones: you take your rest
                 Upon *their knees.*

6   About the Altar with
                          the cherubim at play
                 You now belong:
      A graceful troop! as you're
                          enchanting Heav'n that way
                 With children's song.
      The Good Lord tells you how
                          He makes the winds, the rose,
                 The birds; and so
      No genius on earth,
                          O Little Children, knows
                 What you all know! . . .

7   The secrets that behind
                    the azure veils retire
        You now behold:
    Into your little hands
                    you take the stars (like fire –
        A thousandfold) . . . .
    You, running, often mark
                    with trace of silver ray
        The evening air:
    I think that when I gaze
                    upon the Milky Way
        I see you there.

8   And after all your fun
                    you rush to Mary's arms,
        And she will keep
    Within her starry veil
                    those golden heads . . . She calms
        You all to sleep.
    O charming little imps,
                    how boldly you embrace
        The Lord (and this
    So pleases Him): you dare –
                    He lets you – stroke His Face:
        How kind He is!

9   O Innocents, to try
              on earth to be as *small* –
     That I will do.
  To be a child! . . . the Lord
              asks me to mirror all
     That's seen in you.
  Help me – those charming things
              which in a child one sees:
     Your openness,
  Your lovely innocence,
              your total trust – all these
     May I possess!

10   Lord, well You know I burn
              for what in exile to
     My soul is dear,
  O Lily of the Vale,
              to gather up for You
     Bright lilies here.
  To please You – that is why
              I cherish, and look for
     These buds of Spring:
  In Baptism, on them
              the dew of morning pour:
     Come garnering! . . .

11 O Innocents! may now
                        your troop yet wider range;
                Because my goal's
        To add to it – my joys,
                        my sorrows, in exchange
                For children's souls!
        Among these Innocents
                        I beg to have a place,
                King of the Blest:
        And, Jesus, then, like them,
                        to kiss Your gentle Face
                And be caressed.

Notes

PN 44

28 December 1896, Feast of the Holy Innocents

'. . . ah! don't be afraid to tell Him that you *love Him, even though you have no feeling of love*; that is the way to *force* Jesus to come to your aid, to carry you like a little child too weak to walk.' (Thérèse, letter to Sister Martha, c. June 1897.)

'The Holy Innocents will not be little children in Heaven; they will have only the indefinable charms of childhood. They are represented as "children" because we have a need of pictures to understand spiritual things' (*Last Conversations*, 21/26 May 1897).

It is necessary not to be put off by Thérèse's use of childish expressions and imagery: they cover solid spiritual doctrine. 'To be a child! . . .' (St. 9), in humility and confidence, is central.

St. 11, l. 3 'add to', i.e. 'increase' its numbers.

60. MY JOY!

1 Happiness – people search for it;
  With no success their hunt is crowned.
  For me, it's quite the opposite,
  Here in my heart *is* joy – it's found!
  It's not a joy that blooms and goes,
  Coming to me, it came to stay.
  Delighting, like a fresh spring rose,
  It smiles upon me every day.

2 Really, I'm far too happy, for
  It's my own will I always do!
  How could I *not* be joyous, or
  Not let my gaiety show through?
  My joy is love of suffering,
  And, though with tears these eyes are blind,
  I smile. I'm truly welcoming
  Thorns with the flowers intertwined.

3 When Heaven's blue grows dark, and so
  Seems to have left me cast aside,
  My joy's to see myself brought low –
  To stay within the shade, to hide.
  My joy's, His Holy Will (so dear
  Is Jesus!) – *that* I shall obey.
  And so I live devoid of fear:
  I love the night as much as day.

4   My joy comes from my staying small;
     And when I trip upon a stone,
     I get up quick. For when I fall
     He takes my hand into His own.
     Then, cov'ring Him with my caress,
     To Jesus: 'You're my All' I say.
     I give Him twice the tenderness
     When from my faith He slips away.

5   If sometimes I shed tears – it's been
     My joy that I've been hiding those.
     To give my suff'ring *charms*, between
     A veil of flowers I interpose!
     To suffer silently, so I'll
     Give Jesus comfort – that's my will.
     My joy comes when I see Him smile
     Although my heart's in exile still.

6   My joy . . . is striving that I'll bring
     Children of Heav'n to birth; it is
     A heart aflame, and whispering
     Over to Jesus, often, this:
     'For You (small Brother and Divine!)
     I'll suffer; I am happy to.
     The only earthly joy of mine –
     That I can give delight to You.

7   'Long as I want my life to be
     If that's what You desire, yet, too –
     If it would please You, this from me,
     To Heav'n I'd like to follow You.
     Love's ceaseless fire consumes, from where
     My soul has Home: in Heav'n above.
     It's death? it's life? – I do not care!
     Jesus, my joy's to give You love.'

Notes

PN 45

21 January 1897, Feast of St Agnes

'*Wood* is not within our reach when we are in darkness, in dryness, but are we not at least obliged to throw on small bits of straw? Jesus is indeed powerful enough to keep the fire going by Himself, yet He is glad when He sees us putting on a little fuel; that is a *delicate attention* that pleases Him, and then He throws much wood on the fire . . .'

'. . . when I *feel* nothing . . . then is the moment to look for small opportunities . . . for example, a smile, a friendly word when what I would like to do is to say nothing or wear a bored look, etc. etc. . . . When I have no (such) opportunities, at least I wish to tell Him often that I love Him; that isn't difficult and it keeps the *fire* going. *Even though* it seemed to me that this fire of love had gone out, I would want to throw something on it, and Jesus would then well know how to relight it' (Thérèse, letter to Céline, 18 July 1893).

St. 5, l. 4 'A veil of flowers': a smile. She will not let her suffering show. Thérèse retained her 'joy', her peace deep-down, even when (as at the time this poem was written) she was in immense darkness of soul.

61. TO MY GUARDIAN ANGEL

1   Glorious Guardian of my soul,
You – shining one – in Heaven fly:
Pure flame! your gentle aureole
Burns by the Throne of God on high.
You come to earth *for me*, and how
You light things up! For you descend,
Fair Angel, as my Brother now.
You are my Comforter and Friend.

2   Knowing how weak I am, you take
My hand, and on the road ahead,
Tenderly watchful for my sake,
You clear the stones from where I tread.
You put to me . . . you gently call
For Heaven *only* to enchant –
The more I'm humble and am small,
The more your face is radiant.

3   O spirit who can tráverse space
More quick than sheets of lightning do!
Fly, I implore you, in my place,
To be beside my dear ones too.
Dry, with your wing, their tears – and sing
How good is Jesus; and proclaim
That there is charm in suffering.
And murmur, very low . . . my name.

4   For saving sinners (as I so
            Desire to, short as life may be –
            Fair Angel, they're my brothers) – oh,
            Your holy ardours give to me!
            I've here my sacrifices, and –
            I've nothing more – my poverty:
            With all your bliss in Heaven's Land,
            Offer them to the Trinity.

5   To you: the wealth of Endless Light
            The King of kings has empire at.
            To me: the humble Host of white,
            To me, the Cross – a treasure that!
            The Cross, the Host – ah yes, with these,
            With *your* aid that I thank you for,
            I wait the other life, in peace –
            Its joys, that last for evermore.

Notes

PN 46

January 1897

Thérèse 'had a devotion to the holy angels and particularly to her guardian angel whom she loved to invoke often' (Sister Marie of the Trinity, deposition, 1916).

'Recommend yourself to your Angel Guardian ... Remember that you are to be guided by your Angel like a blind man, who cannot see the dangers of the streets, and trusts entirely to the person who leads him.' (St Aloysius Gonzaga).

For all the purity and power of angels (e.g. stanza 3, lines 1–2), in Thérèse's eyes they lack two great prerogatives which human beings have: as pure spirits they cannot suffer, and they cannot die as martyrs (cf. Poem 4). 'The angels cannot suffer, they are not as happy as I am', Thérèse remarked, a month before her death.

St. 1, l. 6 'light things up'. Thérèse wrote 'm'éclairant', lighting, or enlightening, me.

62. TO THÉOPHANE VÉNARD

Priest of the Foreign Missions, martyred 1861
in Tonkin (Vietnam), aged 31.
Canonised, 1988.

1   Now all the Blest in Heav'n sing out your praise,
Théophane, *Martyr* – like an Angel, too.
Seraphim (thinking of your earthly days)
In angel-hosts, aspire to serving you!
I'm still in exile here, I cannot pour
My voice out with the Blest as I desire:
Like them, however, on this foreign shore,
To sing your virtues now I take my lyre.

2   That hymn was sweet, *your* exile. (It was short,
But how you captured hearts by what you'd say!).
For Jesus, your poetic spirit brought
The ground to blossom where you took your way.
And as your soul was going up at death
Your leaving-song was still as fresh as Spring:
You mumured 'Short this life of mine, a breath;
I'm "going first", to Paradise I wing!'

3   O Happy Martyr! at the torture's height,
In suffering, you *savoured* what befell:
You – suffering for God was a delight –
Knew, smiling, how to die and live as well.
Your slaughterer – should he accelerate
Your death? he asked – straightway your
      answer had:
'The longer is my martyrdom, more great
Its value, and the more I shall be glad!!!'

4   O Virgin Lily! in your Springtime days
The King heard your desires and answered them –
You were a bloom, of whitest fire ablaze:
The Lord desired to pick you off the stem.
You now (no longer in our exiled state –
Full open) plaudits from the Blessèd win!
The Virgin – Rose of Love, Immaculate –
Has smelled your perfume and has breathed it in.

5   Soldier of Christ! ah, now lend *me* your arms,
I'll suffer much for sinners. How I long
To fight, in shadow of your victory-palms –
Protect me! hold me, so that I'll be strong.
These battles, in an endless fight – they form
Assaults upon the Kingdom. For my aim –
For sinners' sake – is taking it by storm:
Not peace the Lord brought us, but Sword and
    Flame!

6   I love that faithless shore-line – in the way
That it was loved so ardently by you.
And if my God should call me to, one day,
How happily I'd hasten there, I too.
Before Him, though, no distances: all things
The universe contains – a pinpoint these!
My feeble love, my little sufferings,
Bless'd by Him, make Him loved across the seas.

7   Ah, may the Lord see me, too, as a flower –
A flower of Spring He'll gather *soon*, then you
May come down here to me, at my last hour –
O Blessed Martyr, I beseech you to!
And, from your love, your purity that glows,
May I, on earth, be set afire by you.
Then I can fly up Heavenwards, with those
Who'll make up your eternal retinue!

Notes

PN 47

2 February 1897, thirty-sixth anniversary of Théophane Vénard's martyrdom.

'One light blow from a sabre will separate my head from my body, like a Spring flower which the Master of the garden picks for his pleasure' (Théophane, letter before his execution).

Jesus 'willed to create great saints who could be compared to lilies and roses, but He has also created smaller ones . . . Perfection consists in doing His will, in being what He wants us to be' (*Aut.*, Ms. A.).

'I know that St Thérèse is known everywhere as the Little Flower and that it was the name she gave herself. It is no doubt presumptuous of me to say that I do not care for it . . . It is a phrase which can create a very false image of her.' Thérèse's character 'was more like an oak tree than a little flower. Her will was of steel.' (John Beevers, Introduction to his translation of Thérèse's autobiography.)

St. 2, l. 8 Days before his execution Théophane wrote to his father: 'Little ephemeral one that I am, I am going first.'

St. 3, ll. 5–6 'accelerate your death', lit., 'shorten your torment'.

St. 5, l. 6 'Kingdom', i.e. the Kingdom of God.

St. 6, l. 1 'faithless shore-line'. Thérèse intended this to refer to the land where Théophane had been martyred, not to the earth as a whole, as I once thought. It is, then (so far as this poem is concerned) not a question of her returning from Heaven to earth, but rather of her desire to be sent from Lisieux to the Carmel of Hanoi, a desire still retained by her in spite of her illness. She explained this in a letter to Père Roulland, adding that Mère Gonzague thought that her, Thérèse's, health was such that if she were sent she would never reach there.

63. MY ARMS

1   From the Almighty I have taken arms;
        I've been arrayed in them by God above!
        Nothing now on, for me, will cause alarms –
        For who could ever part me from His Love?
        Come sword or fire, next *Him* I'll stay serene –
        I'll rush to the arena fearlessly;
        My enemies will know I am a queen –
            A spouse of God is what they'll see!
        Jesus, I'll guard this armour, that I don
        In adoration (which Your eyes arouse):
    Life's close will see me with
               my loveliest garments on! –
        These are my sacred Vows.

2   Poverty – my first sacrifice! you'll be
        Companion till my earthly life is done.
        It's like an athlete in the Games – when he
        Is totally detached . . . *then* he can run!
        Taste, wordly ones (for it's remorse and pain)
        The bitter produce of your vanity.
        In the arena is my joy and gain;
            See there my palms – in Poverty.
        'By violence does one take and bear away
        The Kingdom' (in the Gospel Jesus said):
    Well, Poverty will be
               the Lance of my array,
        The Helmet on my head.

3   Chastity makes me kin to angels, who
     In purity have gained their victory.
     To soar with them one day, I've this to do
     (I, too) – on earth, some fighting's due from me!
     Yes, fight I must, no rest or truce! Record –
     The Lord of lords, my Spouse, I'm fighting for –
     That Chastity (for it's my Heav'nly Sword)
          Of hearts for Him, is conqueror.
     Chastity arms me. It, invincible,
     Makes all my foes give in to me and fly:
And by it I become . . .
                    joy inexpressible! –
               Jesus's Spouse am I.

4   Lucifer – pride-possessed in all his light –
     Still has as blazon 'I will not obey!'
     I blazon, to light up the earthly night:
     'I'll be obedient, always' – *that* I say.
     A holy daring's born in me: elate,
     I'll brave the whole of hell and never yield!
     Obedience – my strength and armour-plate –
          Is, for my heart, a solid Shield.
     That glory only, God of Hosts! My will
     Submissive, all the time, I want to be.
Since one who has obeyed
                    can tell his vict'ries still
               Throughout Eternity.

201

5 If with a warrior's power-in-arms I fight,
 And if like him I struggle valiantly,
 Yet, too, like her whose grace is our delight,
 The Virgin – I would strive, but sing as she!
 You make the strings upon this lyre vibrate
 (This heart within me, Jesus – it's Your lyre)
 To sing of how Your Mercies are so great –
  Sing of their gentleness and fire.
 So, smiling, I will face the bullets' hail –
 My Spouse . . . ah, how Your comfort of me calms!
 I'll die upon the field
    still singing! – for still they'll
  Be held by me, those Arms!

Notes

PN 48

25 March 1897, Feast of the Annunciation

Thérèse of Lisieux 'is fearless . . . She loves *war*. She is a fighter by nature' (Hans Urs von Balthasar, *Thérèse of Lisieux*).

'I made you smile, dear little Brother, in singing of "My Arms"; well, I am going to make you smile again by telling you that when I was a child I dreamt of fighting on battlefields . . . (but) instead of a voice from Heaven inviting me to the fight [like Joan of Arc] I heard in the depths of my soul a voice sweeter and stronger still . . . I understood that my mission was, not to get a mortal being crowned but the King of Heaven loved; to make subject to Him the realm of hearts' (Thérèse, letter to the Abbé Bellière, 25 April 1897).

This poem was written for Marie Guérin (Sister Marie of the Eucharist) on the occasion of her Profession.

St. 5, l. 8 'fire', lit., 'strength' (*force*)

ll. 11–12 In the French, lit., 'In Your arms (*bras*), O my divine Spouse, I shall die singing on the battlefield, Arms (*Armes*, weapons) in hand!' For this translator the temptation to bring both ideas together through the double meaning of 'arms' in English could not be resisted! Jesus's arms are round her; and she in turn (surely) holds on tight to them, as well as to her spiritual weapons.

64. TO OUR LADY OF PERPETUAL SUCCOUR

1   Since I was very young, your picture here
     Has given me delight of heart; I knew –
     Seeing you look at me – you held me dear:
     And I was happy being close to you.

> *Refrain*
> I'll go and see *you* – always! – when I quit
> This foreign shore, O Mary. Ah, but how
>   Good that your picture's here, for it
>   Is my Perpetual Succour – now!

2   When I was well-behaved, obedient,
     You seemed to smile at me: but I would see,
     If sometimes I was naughty . . . well, that meant
     I thought I saw you crying over me.

3   In granting what I simply asked you to,
     A loving Mother, always you would show
     To me – I found this when I looked at you –
     A little taste of Heaven, here below.

4   I feel you make me strong, dear Mother, when
     I'm fighting for my God with battle-sword:
     You know that, at the close of life . . . ah, then
     I'd like to offer *Priests* up to the Lord!

5   O picture, of my Mother up on high,
     You'll be my joy for ever – for you will
     For ever be my treasure . . . Oh! may I
     In my last moments gaze upon you still.

Last refrain
O Mary, I shall sit upon your knee –
At death I shall have flown up to your feet:
All to myself, you'll give to me
Your kisses, Mother – ah, so sweet!

Notes

PN 49

March 1897

'What I came to do in Carmel I declared at the feet of Jesus-the-Host, in the examination which preceded my profession: "I have come to save souls, and above all in order to pray for priests"' (*Aut.*, Ms. A).

The picture referred to in this poem is that of Our Lady of Perpetual Succour (or 'Perpetual Help'). This ancient picture, Byzantine in style, is now in the Church of St Alphonsus Liguori in Rome. It represents the Blessed Virgin holding the Divine Child; the archangels Michael and Gabriel present before Him the Cross and other instruments of His Passion. Renewed devotion to Our Lady under that title was fostered by the Redemptorist Fathers in the nineteenth century.

Thérèse had a facsimile of this picture in her breviary. Sister Marie of the Trinity (for whom this poem was written) felt a great attraction to the picture, and it is her personal thoughts the poem expresses. She entered the Lisieux Carmel on the eve of the Feast of Our Lady of Perpetual Succour 1894, overcoming previous difficulties after praying to the Virgin under that title. She, Sister Marie, is the 'I' in the poem.

Refrain, ll. 1–2 The French, more positively, speaks, not of leaving here but of going to the heavenly shore.

St. 4, l. 2 Thérèse simply says 'When I fight . . . In the combat'.

65. TO JOAN OF ARC

1   When God, the Lord of Hosts ' gave you the
      victory,
   You drove the strangers out, ' made crown'd your
      monarch too.
   Then, Joan, your name became ' renowned in
      history –
   Our greatest conquerors ' all pale compared with
      you.

2   A fleeting glory, though! ' You needed to possess
   That aureole, a saint's ' which never can grow dim,
   Your Love held out to you ' His cup of bitterness –
   You drank; and humankind ' rejected you, like Him.

3   For, in a lightless cell, ' weighed down by heavy
      chains,
   There then were rained on you ' the strangers'
      cruel jeers.
   No friend of yours was found ' to share with you
      your pains –
   None was there to step forth ' and wipe away your
      tears.

4   That darkness in your jail ' more radiance projects
   Than did the Crowning, when ' such high acclaim
      you got!
   The lustre you have *now*, ' in glory, it reflects:
   What was it brought it you? ' Betrayal – that is
      what.

5   If God had not, from love ' unto His Passion come
    And in this vale of tears ' sought death, betrayal,
        thus,
    Our suffering would then ' have been so
        burdensome! . . . .
    Yet now we love it: for ' it's treasure now for us.

Notes

PN 50

May 1897

In France a prayer for the beatification of the Venerable Joan of Arc was being circulated and said at this time.

St. 1, l. 2 'strangers': foreigners, i.e. the English.

66. AN UN-PETALED ROSE

1   First, Jesus, Mary's hands
                made sure you didn't fall:
        Then, on your own,
   You tried, on our sad earth,
             shakily first of all
        To walk alone . . .
  Before You, I would break
             the petals off a rose
        Fresh from the bower –
  So that each little foot
             of Yours, that forward goes
        Rests on a flower! . . .

2   This rose, *un-petaled now*,
               is, Holy Child! that heart
        (The figure's true)
  Which wants to immolate
             itself – in every part,
        Always, for You.
  Fresh altar-roses, Lord,
             are gratified to shine –
        Self-gifts we *see*! –
  Instead of that *I* would
             (this other dream is mine)
        Un-petal me . . .

3   Delightful Child! the rose
                can deck Your Feast-days when
        It's at its height.
  The rose, *un-petaled* though –
                thrown to the wind's will, then
        Blown out of sight!
  That rose gives up itself –
                all artless – that it may
        No longer live.
  Child Jesus! I, to You
                give *my*self up that way –
        Joyously give!

4   Upon such petals then
                one walks without regret:
        And their debris
  Are ornaments by no
                deliberation set –
        This now I see.
  For You, I've strewn my life –
                my future, with what's gone:
        To mortal eye,
  A rose that always will
                be withered from now on,
        I ought to *die.*

5   Supremely lovely Child!
                    for You I ought to die –
              Happily too!
     I'll die to show You I,
                    un-petaled, love You . . . my
              Treasure is You . . .
     Beneath Your baby steps
                    I'll live, while here below,
              In mystery:
     I'll soften, too, Your steps –
                    Your last ones, those that go
              To Calvary!

Notes

PN 51

19 May 1897

By this month it was clear that Thérèse was gravely ill. Her weakness and her pain were to become worse. She now had only four months to live.

'It isn't "death" that will come and seek me, it's the good God. Death is not a phantom, a horrible spectre, as represented in pictures. It says in the catechism that "death is the separation of the soul and the body", that's all it is!' (*Last Conversations*, 1 May 1897).

Her illness advancing, Thérèse expresses in this poem a complete surrender of being and of will to God. She wants only what will please Him. When she was approaching fifteen (she had written in her autobiography) she had, for some time then, offered herself 'to the Child Jesus as His *little plaything* . . . a little ball of no value' that He could do what He liked with (Ms. A).

In the following month, June, she will be ordered by Mère Gonzague to continue her autobiography by writing what became Manuscript C.

St. 3, ll. 7–8 Lit., 'Like it [the rose], I happily surrender myself to You, little Jesus.'

St. 4, l. 5 'For You': lit., 'For Your love', 'for love of You' (*pour ton amour*).

67. *ABANDON'S* THE DELICIOUS FRUIT OF LOVE

L'abandon: *the attitude of a little child*
who has thrown itself into its father's arms.
A 'glorious abandon'.

1   There is on earth a Tree
       That bears a wondrous fruit;
       That grows . . . O mystery! –
       In Heaven is its root.

2   Its shade will never fail
       To keep one safe from harm.
       One will not fear the gale –
       For, there, one can be calm.

3   And from its branches fair
       (The tree is Love) there came
       A fruit, that's sweet and rare –
       Abandon is its name.

4   On earth, that fruit divine
       Has given me content –
       Such joy of heart is mine
       At so divine a scent.

5   This fruit's a treasure when
       I touch it on the tree:
       But tasting it! ah, then
       It's sweeter still for me.

6   It gives me, here below,
       Repose — a sea of peace;
       Unfathomable, so
       That it will never cease.

7   Yes, it alone will give
       Me to Your arms, to rest,
       O Jesus. Thus I live
       The life of Heaven's Blest.

8   *Abandon* — I to You,
       O Spouse Divine! I'll raise
       My eyes: for I pursue
       Only *Your* gentle gaze.

9   As on Your Heart I stay
       To drowse with my Adored,
       I'll smile, and say and say
       Just this: 'I love You, Lord.'

10   A daisy to the sky
       Looks up (red-chaliced one).
       A *little* flowerlet, I
       Half-open to the Sun.

11   And my sweet Sun — You shine,
       O lovely King! — is You
       Who are the Host Divine:
       You've become little too.

12   You've come here, from the Height,
       Celestial Flame whose heat
       Has warmed me! By its light
       Abandon is complete.

13   If creatures *all* desert
Me – well, I'll let them do!
In that, there'll be no hurt
When I am near to You.

14   If You desert me (O,
My Treasure! God) I will –
Deprived of sweetness – show
You I am smiling still.

15   In peace, I will await
Your coming-back, my King –
Not by a note abate
The hymns of love I sing.

16   No, Jesus! I have got
No fear of woes-to-be –
Even the lark can not
Fly higher up than me.

17   Dark clouds? If one could soar
Through them, it's blue above! –
One lands upon the shore
Where reigns the God of Love.

18   I wait in *peace*, to come
To Heaven as an heir.
See, this ciborium –
The Fruit of Love is there!

Notes

PN 52

31 May 1897

'Holiness does not consist in this or that practice. It consists in a *disposition of the heart*, which makes us humble and little in the arms of God, well aware of our feebleness, but boldly confident in the Father's goodness': Thérèse (*Novissima Verba*).

Sœur Thérèse de Saint-Augustin (see note to Poem 1) asked Thérèse, ill but not yet in the infirmary, to write a poem about *abandon*. On publication of the poem after Thérèse's death, its title, *Abandon*, was followed by what purported to be a quotation from that other Thérèse's second patron: '"*Abandon* is the delicious fruit of love" (*St Augustine*).' No-one, however, has been able to find those exact words within St Augustine's works.

St. 1, l. 4 'In heaven is its root'. One is meant to envisage a tree upside-down; roots in heaven, branches and shade on earth. (Like something in a picture by Chagall, the notes in the critical edition aptly and neatly say.)

St. 2, l. 2 'safe from harm', lit., 'nothing could wound', injure (*blesser*).

St. 3 In this stanza Thérèse calls the tree *ineffable* – 'indescribable', beyond description.

St. 10, l. 3 The French also has a double diminutive ('*petite fleurette*', italicized thus).

St. 18, ll. 3–4 The 'littleness' of God in the Eucharist is Thérèse's example and strength.

68. FOR SISTER MARIE OF THE TRINITY

About, as well as for, Sister Marie

1   Lord, You have chosen me ' and since my childhood
    days,
    And I can call myself ' a work-of-love of Yours.
    Would I could pay You back ' in gratitude and
    praise,
    In giving thanks for that ' of which You were the
    cause!
    Poor nothing that I am, ' what have I done for You,
    Dear Jesus, to receive ' advantage of that sort?
    And now! I'm here among ' the royal retinue –
    My God and Beauteous King, ' the virgins of Your
    court.

2   I'm feebleness itself, ' and nothing more, I fear.
    You know it, O my God; ' and yet . . . You know
    this too –
    I have no virtues, yet ' my sole-Beloved here
    Who's captivated me ' – my Jesus, that *is* You!
    When that in my young heart ' was lighted, like a
    flame
    (The name of it is love) ' You asked for it from me:
    And, Jesus, only You ' could satisfy the claim
    Of one who had such need ' to love – and endlessly!

3   When, like a little lamb, ' I'd frolic, and would fail
    To mark, beyond the fold ' the dangers that are
        there,
    Then, Queen of Heav'n, you'd make ' me safe
        inside the vale –
    Unseen, you'd show to me ' a Shepherdess's care.
    And even when I played ' beside a precipice,
    You lifted – even then ' my eyes to Carmel's
        heights.
    To fly to Heaven! . . . first ' (I comprehended this)
    What I would have to love ' were these austere
        delights.

4   Yet, if You cherish, Lord, ' such purity of fire
    As Angel spirits show ' who ride the air above,
    Do you not also love ' – in bloom, above the mire –
    This lily You kept pure ' and holy by Your love?
    If *he* is happy, God, ' the angel as he soars
    On his vermilion wings ' before You – pure to see,
    Here, Angel! on the earth ' my joy's the same as
        yours,
    Such treasure I have now, ' in my virginity!

Notes

PN 53

May 1897

'You want news of [Marie Castel, later Sister Marie of the Trinity,
to whom Thérèse was acting as assistant novice-mistress] . . . I
really believe she WILL STAY . . . (Thérèse, letter to Céline,
18 July 1894).

The title given to this poem on first publication was 'A Lily in the
Midst of Thorns'.

69. WHY I LOVE YOU, MARY!

1   O Mary, I'll now sing ' '*I love you — this is why*';
It's why your gentle name ' brings flutters to my
    heart,
And why the thought of all ' your greatness up on
    high
Could never, to my soul ' a second's fear impart.
If I should gaze on you ' in glory and perceive
Your blaze, that all the saints' ' — all their lights —
    multiplies,
That I'm a child of yours ' I then could scarce
    believe —
Before you, Mary, *then* ' I'd lower dazzled eyes!

2   A mother (that she'll be ' then lovable the more)
Must share her small one's griefs ' — weep, even,
    with him too.
My dearest Mother, here ' upon this foreign shore,
Ah, how your many tears ' attract *this* child to
    you . . .
For when *your life, as in* ' *the Gospel*, I recall,
I dare to look, and then ' approach the one I see:
Believing I'm your child's ' not difficult at all;
I see you — mortal, and ' you're suffering like
    me . . .

218

3   When Heaven's angel came ' to offer you no less
Than *Motherhood* of God ' (whose reign's eternal)
    . . . see!
You, Mary, you preferred ' – what words cannot
    express –
The treasure, kept for Him, ' of your *virginity*.
O Spotless Virgin, I ' see how you mightn't fail
To be more dear to Him ' than where He dwells,
    Above:
Your soul that can contain ' (*Low-lying, gentle Vale*)
Your Jesus – even He, ' that Ocean-flood of
    Love! . . .

4   I love you when you name ' yourself the
    servant-maid
Of God, whom you delight ' by your humility –
Hid virtue, which makes you ' all-powerful . . .
    arrayed
By this your heart attracts ' the Blessed Trinity!
God's Holy Spirit, Love ' came down, and in His shade
The Father's equal Son ' . . . became your little one.
So many sinners were ' to be His brothers made –
Seeing we are to call ' Jesus your 'first-born Son'.

5   Beloved Mother, now ' despite my littleness,
     That same Almighty *I* ' possess in me, like you.
     I see my weakness, but ' it gives me no distress –
     'A mother's treasure' means ' her child has
          treasure too.
     I am your child indeed, ' O Mary! Mother dear;
     Your virtues and your love ' are they not mine?
          and when
     The Host of white comes down ' to rest in my
          heart here,
     Your Lamb believes he comes ' to you – to *your*
          heart then!

6   It's you who make me feel ' it really can be done –
     To follow you, O Queen ' of all the Saints! Ahead
     The narrow road to Heav'n ' you've made a
          well-lit one:
     It's daily little things – ' I see the path to tread.
     O Mary, next to you, ' I love my staying small;
     Of greatness here below ' I see the vanity.
     Your visitation to ' your cousin I recall
     And learn to imitate ' your ardent charity.

7   I listen, raptured there ' O gentle Queen of Heav'n –
     That sacred song your heart ' pours out has now
          begun!
     You teach me to repeat ' the praises you have giv'n:
     To glorify – rejoice ' *in God, your Saviour-Son.*
     Like mystic roses are ' your words of love. They go
     To make all ages sweet ' from what you have
          professed.
     He – the Almighty – *has* ' done great things in you!
          so
     I want to think on them, ' that God may thus be
          blessed.

220

8   Saint Joseph didn't know | what miracle was here.
A *tabernacle*, you | had secrets, then, to keep –
Such Beauty you enclosed! | (See, Joseph standing
    near.)
So humble were you! He, | not knowing, had to
    weep.
Your *silence*, Mary – oh, | how *eloquent!* – to me,
A harmony of sounds | that sweetly thrill and
    move.
It speaks and says 'How great, | all-powerful,
    must be
A soul who simply waits | for help from up above.'

9   O Joseph! Mary! then | you went to Bethlehem.
I see you turned away | – 'no room' at each
    inn-gate.
From all who lived there . . . well, | what help had
    you from them?
Poor strangers get 'no room'; | the place goes to
    the great.
The place goes to the great; | *and yours a stable is –*
That's where the Queen of Heav'n | *has to bring God to*
    birth!
O dearest Mother, you're | so lovable in this!
How great I find you, in | so poor a part of earth.

10   When Love Eternal wrapped ' in swaddling clothes
      I see,
     And, from the Word of God, ' such little cries I
      hear,
     Angelic-spirits then ' no envy rouse in me,
     For, look! their mighty Lord ' is now my Brother
      dear.
     O Mary! – how I love ' you, who upon these
      shores
     Have made bud forth and bloom ' that Flower of
      Heaven there!
     Then, with the Shepherds, Kings ' . . . that listening
      of yours:
     You guarded, in your heart, ' all things with quiet care.

11   With other women who ' have come there, you're
      upon
     The Holy Temple mount. ' I love you, as I see
     You lift Him up, and so ' present to Simeon
     The Saviour of our souls ' . . . he holds Him
      tenderly.
     At first it makes me smile ' to hear the old man
      sing:
     But soon his tones have changed; ' they start me
      weeping, when
     What words of future grief ' his prophesyings
      bring! –
     For he presents to you ' a sword of sorrows then.

12 Up to the evening hours ⎮ of life (O Martyrs'
        Queen!)
      This sorrow-bearing sword ⎮ *will pierce you through
        the heart:*
      Already – to escape ⎮ from Herod's jealous spleen,
      You have to rise and from ⎮ your native soil
        depart –
      As Jesus sleeps in peace, ⎮ wrapped round with
        your veil-folds,
      St Joseph comes and says ⎮ that you must up and
        fly!
      Obedience's *own* ⎮ unveiling one beholds:
      You leave – without delay: ⎮ you never question
        why.

13 Yet, Mary, this I think ⎮ that there in Egypt, and
      In poverty! such joy ⎮ you, even then, are giv'n:
      For, Jesus – *isn't He* ⎮ *the loveliest Native Land?*
      What matters exile, for ⎮ you're still possessing
        Heav'n!
      But in Jerusalem, ⎮ so bitter then . . . distress
      Did – vast as might a sea ⎮ flood in – this joy
        succeed:
      Jesus, throughout three days, ⎮ *hides from your
        tenderness –*
      That, for severity, ⎮ an exile was indeed.

14 At last – what joy – He's found! | with doctors of
        the law;
    And, to the lovely Child | who charms them all,
        one hears:
    'O Son, why did you act | in this way, tell us! Your
    Father and I have been | searching for you in tears.'
    And God, a Child, replies | – how deep the
        mystery! –
    (Your arms stretched out to him) | asks of his
        Mother dear:
    'Why was it that you searched | for me? – did not
        you see
    That I must be about | my Father's business here?'

15 The Gospel tells me next: | in wisdom Jesus grew,
    'Was subject to them' – yes, | submissive then He
        stayed
    (And with what tenderness | to Joseph and to you,
    My heart says): always His | dear parents He
        obeyed.
    And now I understand | the Temple's Mystery
    (The words of this sweet King, | the meaning that
        was hid):
    Mother, your Child desires | that we *example* see –
    Souls in the night of faith | should seek Him as you
        did.

16   Since Heaven's King has willed ˈ that His own
          Mother should
     Be plunged in such a night ˈ its anguish to possess,
     Mary, upon this earth ˈ to suffer, then, is good?'
     'To suffer, *when you love* ˈ *is purest happiness!*' . . .
     Ah, He can take back all ˈ that He has given me
     (No need to *ask* me! – tell ˈ Him that). I do not
          doubt
     That He can hide, but I'll ˈ be waiting, you will
          see! –
     Till all is endless Day ˈ (faith then a lamp put out).

17   At Nazareth your life ˈ (O Mother full of grace!)
     Was poor – you didn't long ˈ for comforts not
          possessed:
     Did transports, raptures come ˈ *or miracles? No trace*
     Of these bedecked you there, ˈ *O Queen of all the Blest!*
     Their number's very great, ˈ your little ones on
          earth;
     To lift up fearless eyes ˈ – this joy to them is giv'n.
     It's by *the common way* ˈ (O Mother beyond worth!)
     That you are pleased to walk, ˈ to guide them up to
          Heav'n.

18   I want to follow you ' each day, my Mother dear –
       To live with you, though I ' still wait my Home
          above,
       I plunge into your heart; ' enraptured, I revere,
       O Mother, seeing there, ' *such an abyss of love!*
       Beneath that mother's-gaze ' I never fear; in turn
       It teaches me to *weep* ' and then *rejoice* with you.
       My pure and holy joys ' you're never going to
          spurn;
       You want to share them, and ' you deign to bless
          them too.

19   At Cana, when you saw ' how worried were that
          pair
       (They couldn't hide it, they ' were running out of
          wine),
       You told your Son, in your ' solicitude and care:
       You hoped for answer from ' the Saviour's power
          divine.
       To start with, Jesus some ' resistance seemed to
          show –
       'Woman, with you and me ' what has this thing to
          do?'.
       What did His Heart-deeps say? ' He calls you
          Mother, so
       A miracle – His first – ' He works there, and for
          you.

20   One day there was a crowd   ' of sinners, being
        taught
    By Him who wanted them   ' to come to Heav'n;
        and when
    They said to Jesus you   ' were on the hill and
        sought,
    Mary, to speak with Him   ' – ah, your Divine Son
        then
    (To demonstrate to us   ' His love's immensity),
    In front of all the crowd   ' upon the hill-side spread:
    'Who is my brother, who   ' my sister, mother? He
    Is that, who does my will',   ' Jesus the Saviour said.

21   O Spotless Virgin, my   ' most tender Mother, at
    The side of Jesus, as   ' you listened to Him . . . see,
    You – not made sad by this –   ' rejoiced He shows
        us that
    Our souls, and here below,   ' become *His family*!
    Yes, you rejoiced that He   ' gives us His own Life
        here –
    The treasures, infinite,   ' of His Divinity . . . .
    How could one fail to love   ' you, Mary, hold you
        dear,
    When seeing all that love,   ' all that humility?

22   As Jesus loves us, so ' you, Mary, love us too:
For our sake you consent ' to separation: thus
That *love is giving all*, ' *is giving self* – that you
Desired to prove, as you ' remained supporting us.
And your vast tenderness ' the Saviour saw. He
      knows
Your tender Mother's heart, ' its secrets! *He has
      giv'n*
To sinners, you to be ' *our Refuge: when He rose*
And left His Cross below ' *to wait for us in Heav'n.*

23   Mary – beside the Cross ' and like a priest! – I see
You offering to God ' the Father up above
(Appeasing Justice there), ' on top of Calvary,
Gentle Emmanuel, ' Jesus, your own heart's-love!
A prophet once said this ' (O Mother, stricken so):
'There is no sorrow like ' Your sorrow . . . .' And
      you would
Stay exiled here! You were, ' for us *unstinting*, O
Queen of the Martyrs! *with* ' *your very heart's
      life-blood.*

24   Saint John's house then becomes ' your only refuge
      – when
Instead of Jesus you'd ' the son of Zebedee.
That told, the Gospels give ' no further detail
      then –
About the Queen of Heav'n ' they tell no more to
      me.
But, silence so profound ' . . . my Mother, does not
      this
Suggest *the Word would wish*, ' *Himself, to manifest*
The secrets of your life ' ah, what a song is His
Eternally to charm ' your *children*, Heaven's Blest!

25   This music I shall hear ⌐ and soon! and will arrive
     In Heav'n, to see you . . . you ⌐ came down to see
       me – how
     You smiled upon me in ⌐ the morning of my life.
     Come, smile on me again! ⌐ for it is evening now.
     No longer do I fear ⌐ your blaze of splendour: I
     Have suffered with you. This ⌐ I am preparing for:
     To sing, upon your knee, ⌐ 'I love you – listen
       why';
     'O Mary! I'm your child' ⌐ I'll sing for evermore!

Notes

PN 54

May 1897

'Do not be afraid of loving the Blessed Virgin *too much*, you will *never* love her enough, and Jesus will be very happy, because the Blessed Virgin is His Mother' (Thérèse, letter of 30 May 1889 to Marie Guérin).

'We oughtn't to say unlikely things, or what we don't know anything about: for example, that when she was very little, at the age of three, the Blessed Virgin went to the Temple to offer herself to God with quite extraordinary feelings of burning love; whereas perhaps she went there very simply to obey her parents' (*Last Conversations*, 21 August 1897).

Mary 'is more Mother than Queen', said Thérèse. This is much quoted. But, by contrast with some today who seemingly cannot overstress the 'ordinariness' of her who bore God Incarnate, Thérèse (who was reacting to an opposite exaggeration, for example, the writer who in 1842 said that the angels and all the blessed, when they see Our Lady, 'hide themselves for shame' as the stars are eclipsed by the sun) was balanced in her expression. 'It is good to speak of (Our Lady's) prerogatives,' she said; rightly adding that 'one should not stop at this' (*il ne faut pas dire que cela*), otherwise people might 'feel a certain estrangement' from someone presented as so lofty and unapproachable.

The Mother of Our Redeemer (though wholly a creature, and redeemed like us, albeit in anticipation of her conceiving and mothering Christ) *is*, as it were, a blaze of light (stanza 1, *ta sublime gloire*): but Thérèse – who knows that Mary is our tender mother also – is not dazzled. Pius XII's Marian Year prayer to Our Lady stresses both facets when it begins: 'Enraptured by the splendour of your heavenly beauty, and impelled by the anxieties of the world, we cast ourselves into your arms, O Immaculate Mother of Jesus and our Mother . . .'

Italics In the French, Thérèse italicizes much in this poem, to stress important points. Those italics have been followed in the translation. (However, the *one-word* italicizations in stanzas 1, 2, 4, 5, 7, 12 and 16 follow Thérèse's general sense rather than any italicization of her own.)

St. 7, l. 1 The setting is that of Mary's visitation to her cousin Elisabeth; the 'sacred song' the Magnificat.

St. 10, l. 7 'Kings'. Thérèse wrote 'wise men'.

St. 16, l. 6 'No need to ask me'. Thérèse uses a phrase which means 'Don't stand on ceremony with me'.

St. 22, l. 2 'separation' alludes to the time after the Ascension when Mary remained on earth.

St. 23, l. 8 To the present translator Thérèse's words brought to mind a moving phrase by Alfred Noyes which refers to the period between the Annunciation and the Birth of Christ: '. . . her whose life-blood once had throbbed in Him'.

ll. 7–8 In a letter to the Abbé Bellière (December 1896) Thérèse wrote of 'martyrdom of the heart'.

St. 25, l. 3 '*You smiled upon me*': a reference to her cure, in 1883, at Les Buissonnets, when a statue of the Virgin appeared to smile at her, penetrating 'to the very depths of my soul' (Ms. A).

70. TO MOTHER MARIE
DE GONZAGUE

Dear Mother, I am adding here
My little word – but what? One thinks,
But hasn't really much idea
When babba-milk is all one drinks! . . . .
And yet, beloved Mother, look –
With joy I offer, for a start,
For putting photos in, this book,
The toques I've made; and my small heart.

Notes

PS 6

21 June 1897

For Mère Marie de Gonzague on her name-day, that of St
Aloysius Gonzaga.

Line 4. Thérèse, ill, was on a milk-diet. She uses the word 'lolo',
baby-talk for 'milk'.

Line 8. 'toques'. Part of the Carmelite habit, worn under the veil.

71. SILENCE, THAT GENTLE TONGUE

1   Silence, that gentle tongue, befits
      The Angel-throng and all the Blest.
      We, too . . . For love-in-Jesus, it's
      How souls, here, love each other best.

2   In *sacrifice* a Carmelite
      Can love; it's never otherwise.
      One day we, drunken with delight,
      Will each love each in Paradise.

Notes

PS 7

Probably June, 1897

Thérèse prefaced this poem with a quotation from St John's Gospel, 15:12: 'This is my commandment, that you love one another as I have loved you.' On a wall in the Lisieux Carmel was written: 'Silence is the language of the angels. Happy the time during which . . . the soul communicates in silence with its God'. Thérèse applies those thoughts to love of one another.

St. 2, l. 3 'drunken'. Thérèse wrote 'enivrées', 'intoxicated'.

233

72. YOU, KNOWING I'M AS SMALL
AS I CAN BE

You, knowing I'm as small as I can be,
Are glad in stooping down, *You* little too:
O white Host, whom I love! Oh come to me,
Come to me, for my heart aspires to You! –
And (after such a favour) grant that I
May die of love – I beg You – and depart . . .
Hear, Jesus, as in tenderness I cry:
    'Come to my heart!'

Notes

PS 8

July 1897

Thérèse wrote this poem on the night of 12–13 July.

Before her Holy Communion, in the infirmary on the morning of 16 July, Feast of Our Lady of Mount Carmel, Sister Marie of the Eucharist (Marie Guérin) sang these lines for her in a 'loud and beautiful' voice: and, after Communion, sang for her Stanza 14 of her poem *Vivre d'Amour* (Poem 26): 'Dying of Love . . . so sweet a martyrdom . . .'

INDEX OF TITLES

INDEX OF FIRST LINES

NOTES TO TRANSLATOR'S INTRODUCTION

Abbreviations

Aut. Thérèse's autobiography, *Story of a Soul* (comprising Manuscripts A, B and C). The quoted extracts are translated by me; but references are given to the following complete translations of the autobiography: *Autobiography of a Saint*, tr. Ronald Knox (London: HarperCollins Publishers, Fount Classics) and *Story of a Soul*, tr. John Clarke, OCD (Washington, D.C.: ICS Publications, second ed., 1976).

LC *Thérèse of Lisieux: her last conversations*, tr. John Clarke, OCD (ICS Publications, 1977). References are to the Yellow Notebook (*Carnet Jaune*) unless otherwise indicated.

LT Indicates Thérèse's own letters in *Letters of St Thérèse of Lisieux*, 2 vols. tr. John Clarke, OCD (ICS Publications, 1982). References are also given to *Collected Letters of Saint Thérèse of Lisieux*, ed. Abbé Combes, tr. F. J. Sheed (London: Sheed & Ward, 1949).

M *A memoir of my sister St Thérèse by Sister Geneviève of the Holy Face* (Céline), tr. The Carmelite Sisters of New York (Dublin: M. H. Gill and Son Ltd, 1959). Céline's '*Conseils et Souvenirs*' including reminiscences by other former novices of Thérèse formed a chapter in later editions of *Histoire d'une Ame*; some of these reminiscences were used in depositions to the Canonical Process of Beatification and Canonization.

'Deposition' in these notes refers to testimony to one or both of the tribunals in the Canonical Process, the Diocesan (1910–11) and the Apostolic (1915–16), pub. Teresianum, Rome.

O'M *St Thérèse of Lisieux by those who knew her*, ed. and tr. Christopher O'Mahoney (Dublin: Veritas Publications, 1975). This contains translations of depositions by fifteen witnesses to the tribunal of 1910–11.

1 John 14:15
2 'I cannot explain this [her physical suffering] except by the ardent desires I have had to save souls' (Thérèse, on the day of her death): LC, 205.
3 Poem 72
4 1 John 4:19
5 Poem 51, St. 5
6 Poem 40, St. 2
7 Poem 57, St. 3
8 Poem 26, St. 3
9 Deposition of Sœur Marthe de Jésus, 1911 (O'M, 227).
10 Poem 20, St. 4 ('pour m'unir à Jésus')
11 *The Eagle and the Dove* (London: Sphere Books Ltd.): St Thérèse of Lisieux, x.
12 Poem 27, St. 10
13 Poem 33, St. 19
14 Poem 39, St. 3
15 Poem 40, St. 3
16 Songs of Songs, 8:5 ('Under the apple tree I raised thee up'.)
17 *Spiritual Canticle,* XXIII, 2; italics mine.
18 Sermon 32 on the Songs of Songs, from *St Bernard's Sermons,* tr. Backhouse (London: Hodder & Stoughton).
19 *Aut.* (Ms. A); Knox, 54–55 (Ch. VII); Clarke, 45.
20 1 Corinthians 2:9
21 1 John 3:2
22 Quoted by Bl. Elizabeth of the Trinity, *Heaven in Faith*, 23. A German theologian has the striking phrase, a 'belonging to one another mutually of God and the creature' in heaven.

23 Introduction to Bruno, *St John of the Cross* (London: Sheed & Ward, 1932).

24 Letter, 27–29 July 1890; LT 109; Sheed, LXXXVII

25 Poem 33, St. 6

26 Poem 26, St. 1

27 Poem 4, lines 63–64

28 Deposition of Sister Marie of the Trinity, 1916 (and 1911, O'M, 235; slightly different wording).

29 Poem 26, St. 14. The frequency with which Thérèse in her poems uses the metaphor of fire is remarkable.

30 Poem 66, St. 2

31 Poem 32, St. 6

32 Poem 43, St. 3

33 Poem 27, St. 53

34 Thérèse's Act of Offering to Merciful Love, 9 June 1895; *Aut.*, Clarke, 276–277. Céline speaks of Thérèse's 'voluntary participation in the Passion of Christ . . . foreseen in her Act of Oblation [Act of Offering] according to the degree willed by Our Lord', M, 83.

35 Blosius (Louis de Blois), *Comfort for the Faint-hearted*, Ch. XXIX; his heading to a quotation from Tauler.

36 Poem 69, St. 5

37 Letter to her sister, Pauline (Sœur Agnès de Jésus, later Mère Agnès), 3 September 1890; LT 114; Sheed, LXXXIX.

38 LC (7 August 1897), 140. By an error of transcription, no doubt, the Clarke translation omits 'without offending the good God' ('*sans offenser le bon Dieu*').

39 Poem 26, St. 6

40 Poem 32, St. 4

41 LC (25 July 1897 – Marie), 239

42 *Aut.* (Ms. C); Knox, 224 (Ch. XXXVI); Clarke, 238.

43 Poem 32, St. 7

43a See Poem 33, St. 13

44 *Aut.* (Ms C); Knox, 194–195 (Ch. XXXI); Clarke, 207–208. Thérèse did not attribute to herself the virtues she practised.

45 2 Corinthians 12:9 (God's power 'is made perfect in infirmity', *ibid.*)

46 Newman's hymn, 'Firmly I believe and truly.'

47 St Teresa of Avila (*Interior Castle*, VI Mansions, X) describes humility as 'walking in the truth'.

48 '... make haste and come down ...' (Luke, 19:5); LT 137, Sheed, CXVI; M, 28.

49 John 3:30

50 Memoir in *Conseils et Souvenirs*

51 The Jerusalem Bible (London: Darton, Longman & Todd).

52 Letter to Céline, 15 October 1889; LT 96, Sheed LXXIV

53 Letter to Céline, 19 October 1892; LT 137; Sheed, CXVI

54 Poem 56, St. 2

55 Quoted by Algar Thorold, *Catholic Mysticism*, 1900, pp. 125 and 145; italics mine.

56 *Novissima Verba*, 17 July 1897; LC (Additional Conversations, July 1897), 257; depositions of Mère Agnès (Pauline), 1910 (O'M, 21) and 1915.

57 Memoir in *Conseils et Souvenirs*.

58 Act of Offering, *op. cit.*; LC (23 June 1897), 67.

59 Deposition of Sister Geneviève (Céline), 1910 (O'M, 125).

60 *Aut.* (Ms. C); Knox, 228 (Ch. XXXVII); Clarke, 242.

61 *Aut.* (Ms. A); Knox, 160 (Ch. XXVI); Clarke, 165.

62 *Aut.* (Ms. A); Knox, 175–176 (Ch. XXIX); Clarke, 180.

63 Poem 67, St. 6

64 Poem 33, St. 20

65 Isaiah 66:12; *Aut.* (Ms. C), Knox, 195 (Ch. XXXI); Clarke, 208.

66 Poem 58, St. 8

67 Poem 26, St. 6

68 Thérèse herself said to Sister Marie of the Trinity: '... be very careful in explaining it, for our "little way", badly understood, could be taken for quietism or illuminism.'

69 R. P. Victor de la Vièrge, OCD (Victor Sion), *Spiritual Realism of St Thérèse of Lisieux* (Thomas More Books Ltd, 1962), 34; a masterly book on Thérèse's spirituality.

70 Poem 11, St. 5

71 One speaks figuratively, of course: 'I never see her run,' the gardener said, of her religious bearing in actuality: deposition of Sister Marie of the Angels, 1911 (O'M, 211). Thérèse's own '*run*, not *rest*' (M, 57) was a metaphor.

72 Deposition of Mère Agnès, 1910 (O'M, 44).
73 Poem 32, St. 4
74 Guy Gaucher, *The Spiritual Journey of St Thérèse of Lisieux*, London: Darton, Longman & Todd (U.S., *The Story of a Life*, San Francisco: HarperCollins Publishers, 1987), Part III, 5.
75 Poem 26, St. 5
76 Poem 51, St. 5
77 Poem 63, St. 1
78 *Ibid.*, St. 5
79 Mid-*word*, indeed: deposition of Sister Marie of the Sacred Heart (Thérèse's sister, Marie), 1910 (O'M, 100). '. . . the pen or the needle was put aside instantly': M, 151.
80 e.g. *Aut.* (Ms. C); Knox, 211–212 (Ch. XXXIV); Clarke, 222–223.
81 *Aut.* (Ms. A); Knox, 106 (Ch. XVI); Clarke, 102.
82 Deposition of Sister Marie of the Trinity, 1911 (O'M, 235). The French here translated 'insignificant' is '*indifférents*'.
83 Memoir in *Conseils et Souvenirs*. 'Nothing sticks to my hands, everything I have, everything I gain, is for the Church and souls': Thérèse, depositions of Mère Agnès, 1910 (O'M, 50), and 1915; LC (12 July 1897), 91.
84 Letter to Céline, 6 July 1893; LT 142; Sheed, CXXI
85 Depositions of Sister Marie of the Trinity, 1911 (O'M, 234) and 1916. On hearing that an author had 'failed in respect and submission to a bishop,' Thérèse stopped reading his books and 'never wished to hear them spoken of again': *The Spirit of St Thérèse de L'Enfant Jésus* (Burns Oates & Washbourne Ltd., 1925), 67.
86 Poem 33, St. 17
87 *Ibid.*, St. 16
88 *Ibid.*, St. 25
89 Poem 6, St. 10
90 *Aut.* (Ms. A); Knox, 103 (Ch. XV); Clarke, 99.
91 *Aut.* (Ms. A); Knox, 104 (Ch. XV); Clarke, 101.
92 *Aut.* (Ms. C); Knox, 202 (Ch. XXXII); Clarke, 214.
93 Poem 33, St. 27 (see translation note underneath poem)
94 'It is so sweet to serve the good God in the night of trial . . .', *Conseils et Souvenirs*: M, 197.

95 *Aut*. (Ms. C), *op cit.,* note 92
96 LC (28 August 1897), 173
97 LC (24 September 1897), 199
98 Letters to Céline, 12 March and 4 April 1889; LT 85 and 87; Sheed, LXI and LXIII.
99 Letter of 4 April, *op. cit.*
100 Letter to Céline, Christmas 1896; LT 211; Sheed, CLXXXII.
101 *Aut*. (Ms. A); Knox, 82 (Ch. XII); Clarke, 77.
102 Guy Gaucher, *The Passion of St Thérèse of Lisieux*, tr. by Sister Anne Marie Brennan, OCD, Pub., St Paul Publications 1989.
103 An earlier record (*Novissima Verba*) has: '. . . never asked the good God for suffering.' See also LC, 290 (letter of Sister Marie of the Eucharist – Marie Guérin – to her father, 27 August 1897).
104 LC (26 August 1897), 169
105 LC (11 August 1897), 145
106 Poem 48, St. 4
107 Poem 34, St. 7
108 Poem 25, St. 2
109 *Aut*. (Ms. A); Knox, 148 (Ch. XXIV); Clarke, 149.
110 Poem 44, Refrain 2
111 Poem 60, St. 5
112 Sister Martha reports Thérèse as having said once: '. . . what a joy it is to suffer for someone you love!' (deposition, 1911, O'M, 219); and see Poem 69, St. 16.
113 e.g. 175 (30 August 1897); 184 (5 September 1897)
114 *Spiritual Canticle*, IX, 6
115 LC (13 July 1897), 95
116 Poem 26, St. 9
117 Song of Songs, 2:10–12
118 LC (4 July 1897), 73
119 LC (30 September 1897), 205; deposition of Mère Agnès, 1910 (O'M, 68).
120 LC (30 September 1897), 206. LC, Céline, 230, and also Pauline's (Mère Agnès's) deposition, 1915, have 'I wouldn't want to suffer less!'

121 LC (30 September 1897), 206; depositions of Mère Agnès, 1910 (O'M, 69) and 1915.

122 Poem 14, St. 18

123 LC, 102; see also LT 254; Sheed, CCXXV.

124 Hans Urs von Balthasar, *Thérèse of Lisieux*, tr. Donald Nicholl (London: Sheed & Ward, 1953), 31; later edition, *Two Sisters in the Spirit: Thérèse of Lisieux and Elizabeth of the Trinity* (San Francisco: Ignatius Press, 1992), 74–75. I have been greatly indebted to that book in the writing of the present Introduction (though I dare to be in less than total sympathy with just a few of its conclusions).

125 e.g. deposition of Sister Marie of the Trinity, 1911 (O'M, 230).

126 Of the writers in English who have noticed the poems, some have summarily dismissed them. Even the admirable John Beevers (*Saint Thérèse, the Little Flower*, Tan Books and Publishers Inc., Rockford, Illinois, 1976, Ch. 5) says that they are 'quite without distinction'. Frances Parkinson Keyes (*Written in Heaven*, Clonmore & Reynolds Ltd., Dublin, 1946, Ch. IX) praises their 'rhythmic quality', 'fluency' and 'grace'.

127 An exception is Poem 69, where I follow Thérèse's italicization closely.

Catechism of the Catholic Church, quoted in Foreword and Translator's Introduction, is published by Geoffrey Chapman, London, 1994.

John Beevers' translation of St Thérèse's autobiography (introduction quoted on page 199) is published by Image Books, Doubleday, New York, 1989.

The quotation from John Beevers on page 100 is from *Saint Thérèse, the Little Flower* (Tan Books and Publishers Inc., Rockford, Illinois, 1976).

The quotation from Sister Teresa Margaret, DC, on page 136, is from *I Choose All* (Fowler Wright Books Ltd., Tenbury Wells, 1964).

The quotation from Alfred Noyes on page 230 is from the poem *The Assumption* in *A Letter to Lucian and other Poems* (London: John Murray, 1956).